Teachers Working Together
for School Success

D1052245

To: My father and mother
Two people who always believed in education for their children
even though their opportunities were limited. Dad, your belief in
me is the driving force behind my motivation even though you
are no longer with us.

Teachers Working Together

for School Success

Mario C. Martinez

CORWIN PRESS
A Sage Publications Company
Thousand Oaks, California

For information:

Corwin Press
A Sage Publications Company
2455 Teller Road
Thousand Oaks, California 91320
www.corwinpress.com

Sage Publications Ltd.
1 Oliver's Yard
55 City Road
London, EC1Y 1SP
United Kingdom

Sage Publications India Pvt. Ltd.
B-42, Panchsheel Enclave
Post Box 4109
New Delhi 110 017 India

Printed in the United States of America

Library of Congress Cataloging-in-Publication Data

Martinez, Mario C.
Teachers working together for school success / by Mario C. Martinez.
    p. cm.
Includes bibliographical references and index.
ISBN 1-4129-0612-1 (cloth) — ISBN 1-4129-0613-X (pbk.))
    1. Teachers—Professional relationships—Handbooks, manuals, etc.
2. Educational leadership—Handbooks, manuals, etc. I. Title. e.
LB1775.M44 2005
371.1—dc222   2004007250

This book is printed on acid-free paper.

04   05   06   07   08   10   9   8   7   6   5   4   3   2   1

Acquisitions Editor:	Faye Zucker
Editorial Assistant:	Stacy Wagner
Production Editor:	Julia Parnell
Copy Editor:	Marilyn Power Scott
Proofreader:	Penny Sippel
Typesetter/Designer:	C&M Digitals (P) Ltd.
Indexer:	Michelle Nilson
Cover Designer:	Anthony Paular

Contents

Preface

I wrote this book because of the feedback I received from the many teachers who attended my seminars and courses that deal with issues of teamwork, interaction, conflict resolution, and leadership. These are topics that are regularly and appropriately aimed at the administrative audience, but teachers at the primary and secondary levels have communicated to me that such topics are equally critical for them. Two years ago, I decided to act on the advice that I should write a book so that more teachers could access the tools from my teachings.

Studies have long shown and researchers have come to understand that people working in the same organization influence one another's attitudes, thoughts, feelings, and even performance. In the late 1960s, Frederick Roethlisberger (1969/2003) wrote that most of us want the satisfaction that comes from being accepted and recognized as people of worth by our friends and work associates. These same conclusions are as applicable to schools and the teachers who work in those schools as to any other organization. More than ever, teachers must work together to address a range of issues, from classroom pedagogy to campus improvement. Teachers can thrive in their school environments if they combine their expertise in the classroom with the interpersonal skills necessary to build a collegial environment.

In Chapter 1, the case is made that teachers need a resource to help build collegiality. There are other factors that contribute to a successful school, but few resources exist that provide tools to help teachers productively interact and work with others. In this chapter and all others, the examples, illustrations, and assessments draw on experiences from the field of education.

In Chapter 2, the language of leadership is cast in a light that is applicable to every teacher. The ideas of leadership in this chapter become manifest through exercises and self-assessments so that teachers may apply these ideas to themselves and their schools.

In Chapter 3, the concepts from personality psychology offer opportunities for teachers to gain insight into their own behaviors and actions as well as those of their colleagues and administrators.

Chapter 4 is reserved for the all-important topic of conflict resolution, because the question is not whether conflict will happen but when it will happen and how you will handle it.

The insights offered by Chapters 3 and 4 are complementary to the topic of teamwork, which is the focus of Chapter 5. The effectiveness of a team is enhanced when its members know how to communicate with different personalities and have different options for dealing with conflict.

Chapter 6 concentrates on the teacher-administrator relationship, and it is here that a working knowledge of different leadership styles can help you work more productively with the formal leaders in your schools.

Chapter 7 is critical because it asks you to think about yourself as a teacher, both inside and outside the classroom. All of the chapters prior to this self-assessment serve the purpose of helping you discover yourself and how you work with colleagues and administrators so that you can more easily assess yourself honestly and accurately.

Chapter 8 pulls the book together and directly states the main message: Everything in the book is meant to be a tool to help teachers improve themselves and their professional relationships.

A side note, but one which I find particularly important, is that each and every chapter is as applicable to our personal lives as our professional lives. I do not believe that we can completely separate our professional and personal lives, because each affects the other. It is my hope that you will find application in both of these overlapping spheres.

Acknowledgments

I am grateful to many people for the completion of this book. First, I would like to thank Faye Zucker at Corwin for her belief in this idea. Faye encouraged me throughout the entire process and never gave up on the idea of producing such a resource for teachers. Her enthusiasm for the project was a tremendous source of motivation. Michelle Nilson not only edited the first draft of the manuscript and created the index, but she was bold enough to tell me when something just didn't sit right. Maria Luisa Gonzalez and Gary Ivory, from New Mexico State University, were great sources of moral support, and for that I thank them.

Last, to my wife, Sara R. De Martinez, whose support for my endeavors and belief in my abilities have never wavered, I am most grateful.

Corwin Press extends its thanks to the following reviewers for their contributions to this book:

Michelle Barnea, Educational Consultant, Millburn, NJ

Nancy Brennan, New York State Education Department, Albany, NY

Diane Holben, Saucon Valley High School, Hellertown, PA

Steve Hutton, Elementary School Principal, Villa Hills, KY

Kim Truesdell, University of Buffalo, NY

About the Author

Mario C. Martinez is Associate Professor in the Department of Educational Leadership at the University of Nevada Las Vegas (UNLV), where he teaches courses in leadership, human relations, and organizational theory. Prior to joining UNLV, he was an Assistant Professor in Educational Management and Development at New Mexico State University. His career also includes time at the Hewlett Packard Corporation as a financial analyst and at the governor's office in the state of Arizona as a strategic management officer.

He also owns MCM Consulting, which is primarily a seminar and speech delivery company, with seminar topics that deal with leadership and relationships in the workplace. His array of career exposures has contributed to his multidisciplinary approach to thinking pragmatically about professional development, evident both in this book and in his seminars and speeches.

His research has been concentrated in the areas of state educational policy, the organizational structures of state educational systems, and the change and management of those systems. He has a PhD from Arizona State University and an MBA from the University of Texas at Austin.

CHAPTER ONE

Successful Teachers, Successful Schools

The relationship between and among professionals in any organization is critical to its success. A successful school is one in which teachers work well together and with their administrators. McLaughlin and Talbert's (2001) study of high school teachers found that collegial support and interaction influence how teachers feel about their jobs and their students. These authors found that collegiality also influences the motivation and career commitment of teachers and the extent to which they are willing to modify classroom practice.

BUILDING QUALITY RELATIONSHIPS

School collegiality concerns the quality of the relationships between and among professionals in a school environment. Few resources directly help teachers build the human relations skills necessary to build a collegial school environment. Most books, training sessions, or college coursework in this area are aimed at the administrative audience. The majority of development and growth opportunity for teachers addresses curriculum and instruction and how teachers can create effective learning environments inside the classroom. While administrative effectiveness and classroom excellence are critical to school success, so too is school collegiality, as shown in Figure 1.1. *Teachers Working Together for School Success* focuses on the tools

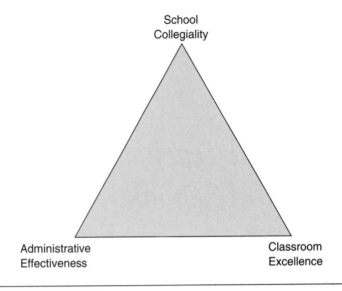

Figure 1.1   Successful Schools

that teachers need to improve school collegiality, thereby providing a resource in an area that has received relatively little attention.

COLLEGIALITY FOR PERSONAL SATISFACTION

Today's teachers must interact with each other more than ever before. The traditionalist claim is that interaction among teachers is of little consequence since the majority of teacher time is spent in the classroom. This claim is no longer accurate. Teachers certainly continue to derive tremendous satisfaction from their classrooms, and they still spend a majority of the day in classrooms. Interaction among teachers has steadily risen, though, and as McLaughlin and Talbert (2001) have convincingly demonstrated, collegiality greatly impacts teachers' morale, happiness, and satisfaction. A collegial school environment is one in which teachers are able to

- Work well with other teachers;
- Work well with administrators;

- Manage conflict with others, including teachers, administrators, parents, and students; and
- Match their educational strengths and preferences with an appropriate school.

COLLEGIALITY FOR SCHOOL IMPROVEMENT

The majority of teachers today, whether at the primary or secondary level, are expected to work with other teachers, coordinators, or administrators at some point during the school year. Teachers may team teach or participate in schoolwide initiatives or campus improvement plans. The success of a new reading program in an elementary school or the installation of a technology lab in a high school both depend on the technical and interpersonal skills of teachers. These are just a few of the many examples whereby success depends on effective working relationships among teachers.

Collegiality contributes to every successful change, and effective administrators purposely draw on the expertise of teachers to discuss or implement new initiatives and programs. And if a change were to be implemented without teacher input, concerns about that change can be most effectively expressed by teachers with strong interpersonal skills. Schools with strong collegial environments are better able to assess and implement changes than schools with weak collegial environments.

Collegial relationships among teachers are a prerequisite for school improvement and make knowledge sharing and innovative practice possible (Fullan, 2001). The success of broad school change also improves when faculty and administrators work well together. In one southwestern state, this working relationship was largely responsible for a middle school successfully transforming into a magnet school. Today, the demand for the art and science curriculum at the school is so high that enrollment is determined by lottery.

An organization cannot realize its full potential without clear and cooperative interaction among employees. This is also true for schools. In the words of one staff development specialist, "children cannot effectively learn until adults effectively get along." Topics of leadership, teamwork, change, and conflict resolution are not just reserved for administrators. School success depends on every teacher's ability to work with others.

COLLEGIALITY CAN BE LEARNED

People in general, whether in social or work situations, are influenced by their relationships with others (Aronson, 1992). In one of the classic studies in organizational behavior, Roethlisberger (1969/2003) found that worker satisfaction and productivity are influenced by social interaction. Teachers make important career decisions based on collegiality or whether there is positive social interaction in their schools. In the best case, collegiality is high and teachers are fulfilled in their careers. In too many other cases, teachers leave the profession because of difficulty with coworkers and administrators, not because they dislike teaching.

Clyde was a very effective teacher and coach in a large junior high school. After nearly ten years of exemplary service to the school and the district, he quit teaching and took a job as a financial consultant. This was a great loss for the children. Clyde loved teaching kids and even volunteered for committee work on a regular basis, which added to his teaching and basketball coaching duties. During the last two years of his teaching career, he felt that communication among teachers and between teachers and administrators was ineffective. The town Clyde lived and worked in was very small, so he chose not to transfer to another school but to begin another occupation. People in every profession leave their jobs for similar reasons—the people they interact with, not the actual job.

Teachers who work in poor school climates can easily lose sight of why their jobs are important. It is hard to be satisfied and happy in a teaching career when people do not get along. The good news is that there are things that every teacher can do to strengthen collegiality. Working with different teachers and administrators requires skills, and these skills can be learned.

Collegiality is important in any organization, as evidenced by the millions of dollars business and government managers spend to train their professionals to improve working relationships. *Teachers Working Together for School Success* is for teachers who have a dual concern for the classroom and the well-being of their schools.

If you are a teacher who has achieved mastery in the classroom, it is likely that your willingness to contribute extends beyond your classroom. You are in an opportune position to build the skills taught in this book. If you are a teacher just learning your craft, you may also be interested in building collegiality if you can simultaneously master the demands of the classroom.

Evans (1996), an expert on school change, says there are naysayers, who he calls *Cryogenics* (p. 274), who are not open to learning new things. They are not committed to new skill development. Cryogenics complain about inservice sessions, mandatory staff development days, and even faculty meetings. Other teachers are what Evans refers to as *Red Hots*. These teachers are hungry for and receptive to new knowledge and information that will help build successful schools and classrooms. They are eager to grow, to improve, to change, and to learn. Teachers who have retained their natural curiosity for learning will find this book a useful guide for self and school improvement.

CONCLUSION

Every chapter in this book has already found real-life application for teachers across all grade levels. All of the information, assessments, and lists throughout the book have been delivered to teachers in various settings: at seminars, full-day inservice sessions, conferences, and college classrooms. The feedback from the many teachers who have already applied this material is that it is needed, it works, and it is fun to learn.

A successful school is built around teachers who are successful inside and outside the classroom. Every teacher is either contributing to collegiality or presenting barriers to achieving it. If you embark on a learning experience to build collegiality in your school, you will help build a successful school, and it will also make you better in the classroom. Skills in this area can reinforce the momentum your school already has or help improve a negative situation. Either way, if you are willing to build skills to improve collegiality, you will be making it easier for children to learn since you will be contributing to a positive school environment. People working together are more effective than a collection of individuals working alone.

CHAPTER TWO

The Leadership Mindset for Teachers

Concepts in leadership books are often difficult to apply. Common advice such as "have a vision," "lower your resistance to change," and "productively confront conflict" fill the pages. No one would argue with the wisdom of such counsel. The problem is that such general advice only tells readers *what* to do but not *how* to do it. Further complicating the picture is that most of the stories and examples in these books are about national public leaders, historical figures, and tycoons. Local stories of leadership also tend to focus on the few, the powerful, or the rich. Newspapers report on the latest efforts by the state's governor to transform education, or perhaps we read about a new initiative championed by the capable leadership of a district superintendent. All of these accounts are motivational and create a desire to positively influence other people—to lead them— but the question remains: How can teachers be leaders in their schools?

MISCONCEPTIONS ABOUT LEADERSHIP

The first step to move from general leadership advice to practical application is to realize that leadership is not reserved for the few. Leadership is not exclusively the realm of those who are "born" with it. Carlyle's (1841/1994) early-1800s studies of leadership concluded that leaders were born not made. For many people, this thinking is perpetuated by leadership books that focus on the famous and powerful. In the latter part of the 1800s, a social scientist named Herbert Spencer (1884/1994) challenged the belief of born leadership. Unfortunately, Spencer adopted a different and opposite view of leadership. He argued that leadership was not at all about an individual. In any school, business, or nation, someone has to be in charge at any given point in time. Those who happen to be in positions of leadership when times are good get all the credit; those who happen to be in positions of leadership when times are bad get all the blame. According to Spencer's reasoning, if a school superintendent resides over a district during good times, it is unlikely that the superintendent had anything to do with creating those good times. If a teacher has a successful school year with students and colleagues, Spencer's extreme view would be that this success had little to do with the teacher.

TEACHERS AS LEADERS

If teachers believe that leaders are born or that only circumstances dictate success, then there is little room to exercise or develop leadership. But teachers *can* exercise leadership and should not adopt any extreme view about it. Leadership is most applicable to teachers when it is thought of in terms of influence. There is little question that every person has some influence over others. Leadership expert John Maxwell (1998) has said that the average person, in his lifetime, affects either directly or indirectly, some 10,000 people. Teachers have exposure to more people than the average person. That means a teacher affects more than 10,000 lives.

If teachers influence students, fellow teachers, and even administrators, how does their influence translate into leadership? Heifetz (1994) writes that leadership is about influence, and influence is mediated through activity. We are all engaged in activity, and our activity influences other people, for better or worse. For Heifetz, leadership results when one's activity positively influences others.

Activity has to do with the things that you think, say, and do. Does your activity positively influence others? If it does, you are exercising leadership. As an example of activity and influence, think about a teacher's activity at an inservice training session. Some teachers approach inservice sessions with enthusiasm, others with disdain. Suppose one teacher is saying negative things about the coming session and is constantly frowning. Some common remarks might include, "I don't know why we have to be here when classes start in two days and there is so much to do" or "This is such a waste of time." The distracting teacher is a naysayer, and his or her actions do not have a positive influence on other teachers at the inservice. Other teachers might start thinking that maybe this session is a waste of time because of the negative teacher's influence. By contrast, another teacher may view the inservice as a chance to exchange ideas and learn new things. This teacher is not afraid to express enthusiasm for the session and positively contribute when the presenter asks questions and seeks participation. Other teachers who wanted to ask questions are no longer as reserved because of the lead the first teacher has taken in creating a positive experience. The enthusiastic teacher has positively influenced others and has shown leadership.

Your Personal Leadership Portrait

An individual's activity is governed by a set of personal qualities. Evaluating personal leadership influence, then, is a matter of discovering what qualities drive your activity. This discovery is a two-step process. Ironically, to create your personal leadership portrait, it is useful to first think about someone else. Read and respond to items 1 and 2 in the following list.

1. Identify a teacher or administrator who has positively influenced your life. This should be someone you currently admire as a colleague or have known during your teaching career. This is someone you consider a leader.

2. Write words and phrases in the top box of Figure 2.1 that describe this person. What are the qualities that made this person a leader, in your opinion? Take five to ten minutes to complete this part of the exercise.

The next part of the exercise requires you to read and respond to items 3 and 4.

3. Think about yourself. What are your leadership strengths (as a teacher, coordinator, administrator, or other professional position you hold)? Write down the words, phrases, or qualities that describe

your leadership strengths in the left-hand box of Figure 2.1. Take five to ten minutes to complete this part of the exercise.

4. What are your weaknesses (as a teacher, coordinator, administrator, or other professional position you hold)? Write down the words, phrases, or qualities that describe your weaknesses in the right-hand box of Figure 2.1. Take five to ten minutes to complete this part of the exercise.

The top part of Figure 2.1, which contains attributes of a leader you admire, paints a picture of what you consider a strong, ideal leader. If you are doing this exercise with others, compare your lists. Here are words and phrases (in no particular order) that teachers and administrators typically write down to describe a leader they admire:

- Honest
- Good listener
- Organized
- Dependable
- Confident
- Deals effectively with others
- Has integrity
- Fair
- Hardworking
- Enthusiastic
- Ethical
- Trustworthy
- Competent

When people are asked to generate a list of admirable leadership qualities, their lists generally look the same, whether they work in education, business, or government. Also notable in the above list is that the word "competent" is the only quality directly related to technical ability or specific job competency. Although the list does not reflect an order of importance, competence is not usually the first attribute that people think of when they describe effective leaders. Evans (1996) believes that technical and nontechnical training are both important in the leadership of change. Yet Evans postulates that it is the nontechnical skills that determine how successful the teacher or administrator will become. Nontechnical skills are at the core of leadership activity, and most words people use to describe effective leaders have little to do with technical ability.

Qualities of an Effective Leader

My Strengths	My Weaknesses

Figure 2.1   Leadership Assessment

Questions 3 and 4 help you develop a personal leadership portrait. Every teacher's list of strengths and weaknesses will be different. As you compare your list of strengths to the list of attributes describing an admirable leader, you may discover that you have many attributes of leadership that help you positively influence others. Conversely, there may be some weaknesses you have identified that are preventing you from being more effective as a leader.

Improving Strengths and Weaknesses

You can apply the lessons of this exercise by identifying two qualities from your list of strengths or weaknesses that you would like to improve. The areas for improvement do not necessarily have to come only from your list of weaknesses. You could identify two items from your list of strengths or two items from your list of weaknesses. You could also identify one item from your list of strengths and one from your list of weakness. The important thing is to decide what attributes from either list will help you be more successful in your job and school environment.

The purpose of the leadership assessment in Figure 2.1 is not solely to identify weaknesses and turn them into strengths. That might be the case for some people, but it is not the rule. We have been programmed to focus on weaknesses because of job evaluations. Administrators typically perform an evaluation and focus on the teacher's weaknesses. The teacher is then urged to improve the weaknesses. That is one approach to evaluation. The other option is to make your existing strengths even better. Handy (1994) urges us to work on our strengths and forget about our weaknesses. Handy believes that we will only reach true excellence by improving our existing strengths; working on our weakness will only get us to average performance. This is certainly a challenge to conventional practice, but it may be applicable to you. However, if you recognize a certain attribute as a weakness and it is critical for job performance and school improvement, you should seek improvement in that area. For example, every teacher needs a good measure of organization. If you are not organized, you may be unduly stressed, impatient with other teachers, and unnecessarily confrontational. This type of behavior (activity) has a negative influence on others and decreases your ability to exert leadership influence. If your lack of organization is causing such problems, you may need to strengthen your organizational skills.

It is important to identify a small, select number of areas for improvement from Figure 2.1 instead of trying to improve in every area. If you identify twenty areas to improve, it is unlikely that you will make progress on any of them. Change experts say it this way: Too many changes happening at once dooms all the changes to failure (Goodstein & Burke, 1995). This is true for individuals as well as organizations. The purpose of this book is to be realistic and practical. Identifying two critical areas instead of twenty is a strategy that forces focus and thus encourages true change and application. Write down, in the spaces below, the two qualities from Figure 2.1 that you would like to improve:

Quality 1:_____

Quality 2:_____

The final step is action. Identifying an issue is half of the solution; initiating action is the other half. Answer the three questions that follow to help you identify what you need to do to start improving in the areas you have identified. Answer each question for the two areas of improvement you identified in Chapter 2.

1. Does anybody else need to be involved or informed of my decision to work on this strength or weakness?

It may be that your administrator needs to know about your decision to improve in a certain area. Perhaps this is because it has been identified as an area of strength or weakness that is important to the school. Maybe your administrator needs to know about this decision because you will be asking for resources. An improvement may also involve another person if you currently know someone who is strong in the area for which you seek improvement. It may be that this person can act as a resource, which leads to the second question.

2. What resources do I need to work on this strength or weakness?

You may need to attend a seminar, a conference, or some sort of training. If you have seen printed resources that address your targeted area of improvement, commit time to review some books or ask people for suggestions so that you can identify the proper resource. Maybe the resource you need most is time—yours or that of another person. There are many simple actions that you can identify to help you start improving in the areas you designated.

3. What can I do right now to get started?

Time is an issue for most people. If you need time to address your targeted area, prioritize your professional and personal activities and designate time periods to work on the areas you have identified. Scheduling and organization are important. It is not usually possible to work on a goal in one big chunk of time, so the best strategy is to work on it over a period of time. If you need the time of a mentor or a knowledgeable person, schedule some time with this person. If you have identified an important book, buy the book and read it. The majority of people who buy a book only read the first 10 or 15 pages. If they read the entire book, they may view the book as the ultimate answer to their problems rather than a tool that needs to be thoughtfully applied, given their situation. In the end, if you believe a book is going to give you useful information, commit to reading it and use it as a resource rather than an ultimate solution. If you believe you need specific training, ask your administrator to support that training and then schedule a date to attend it. These are all examples of action.

You will be more effective in your job and with your colleagues if you improve in the two areas you have identified. The level of application you find in this chapter is largely determined by how you answered the three questions for each improvement item. If you have answered the three questions for each area of improvement, and if you follow through on the third, then you will improve teacher collegiality in your school. As you read through each chapter in this book, you will discover tools to help you increase your leadership influence. This influence will help you positively contribute to teacher collegiality. Periodically revisit the two improvement areas you identified in this chapter. If something from a particular chapter strikes you as important, it may be a tool to help you improve in your designated area. If something from a particular chapter better defines a new area for improvement, then replace one of the items from your previous list. Feedback from other people is also valuable because it may help you identify areas you wish to target. Last, do not hesitate to change your list to reflect new thoughts and ideas that surface as you read, but keep your list of improvements to only two areas.

CONCLUSION

You now have a starting point to increase your leadership effectiveness as a teacher. The next chapters will equip you with the tools to build collegiality in your school. This requires that you learn about yourself as well as others. When you learn more about yourself, you also gain insight into how other people perceive you. This will help you further clarify your strengths and weaknesses. When you learn more about others, you learn how to work together to improve your school.

CHAPTER THREE

Teacher to Teacher

Personality and Communication

S chool-related problems can often be traced to problems between people. One teacher may have a problem with the way another teacher communicates. Each teacher communicates differently because each has a different personality, and personality influences communication and the way we think, act, and behave. For example, a problem between two teachers may arise in a committee meeting while the group is discussing how to implement a new instructional practice. One teacher may believe that more discussion is needed and that the practice should be phased in, but another teacher thinks it should be implemented immediately. Each teacher requires a different level of detail about the new instructional practice and an individual idea of how fast it should be implemented. It is likely that these differences have a lot to do with each teacher's personality. Some people require a good deal of detail and feel it would be unwise to immediately implement a new instructional program without more information. Others may be more tolerant of taking a risk, so immediate implementation may seem like a good idea.

UNDERSTANDING PERSONALITY INCREASES COMPATIBILITY

School collegiality is strengthened when faculty understand each other and know how to effectively communicate with each other.

A teacher who understands the nuances of different personalities understands how to meet the needs of other teachers and navigate through the complexity of problems that can arise because of individual personality differences. Problems attributed to personality differences affect how teachers feel about their jobs, colleagues, and even classrooms. Work relationships are also important because people develop many personal relationships through work. Buckingham and Coffman (1999) found that one important ingredient that contributes to a happy and effective employee is whether that employee has a best friend at work. Buckingham and Coffman's work points to the positive social interactions that every person desires, many of which are fulfilled in the workplace.

Compatibility between and among faculty is largely about effective interaction between different personality types. In this chapter, you will learn about four personality types. You will take an assessment to learn more about your own personality. Each personality type has certain preferences, needs, wants, strengths, and weaknesses. As you go through the assessment and identify the characteristics of your personality, you may discover that the two areas of improvement you identified in Chapter 2 are linked to the strengths or weaknesses of your personality type.

The foundation of school collegiality lies in how teachers get along and work together. Those who learn about their own and their colleagues' personalities can work together more effectively. Teamwork and conflict resolution are also influenced by the personalities of the people who are working on a team or trying to resolve a conflict, two topics that will be discussed in Chapters 4 and 5.

An equally important benefit for teachers who learn about personality and interaction is that the knowledge can be applied to multiple settings, with children or adults. Children, parents, teachers, and administrators all have different personality types. A teacher who has knowledge of personality types can respond and communicate more effectively with children in the classroom, parents in a conference, or administrators in a meeting.

ASSESSING YOUR PERSONALITY

The subject of personality has drawn considerable research interest. This interest gave birth to an entire field of study called *personality psychology* (Hunt, 1993). There are many instruments that have been used over the years to help people identify their personality types. Some instruments identify sixteen possible types, others as few as four. Most are conceptually similar even though the terms they use to describe different personalities may vary. Many of these instruments have withstood statistical testing and are deemed valid and reliable indicators of personality. These assessments owe their development to the work of early personality psychologists. Hunt identifies the work of early twentieth-century psychologists Hans J. Eysenck and Raymond Cattell, who independently tested for relationships among multiple traits that could describe distinct personality factors. The work of these psychologists was influenced by Carl Jung, who divided people into categories of extroversion and introversion, as well as thinking and feeling types.

From a practitioner's standpoint, the application and implication of personality types is evident. Accurate identification of different personality types can help teachers gain conscious insight into how different people think, act, and behave. A study of personality theory is also one of self-discovery, whereby you learn about your personality type and how it influences your relationships.

Salespeople have long used personality theory to aid them in their businesses. The classic and sometimes exaggerated claim is that salespeople apply this knowledge to gain insight into the prospects' personalities by an initial two-minute conversation. If salespeople perceive that prospects are direct, no-nonsense persons, they may get right to the point, briefly explain the most prominent features of their products, and inform the prospects of the price. They surmise that these particular prospects do not care about chatting and exchanging stories. Other prospects, who like to know who they are buying from, may want more interaction with the salesperson. These prospects may want to sit down and talk a bit longer to see if they can trust the salespeople and everything they are saying. The salespeople would obviously handle prospects differently, based on their personalities.

The application of personality theory is not limited to the business world. There have been great strides in applying the concepts behind personality theory to educational environments. Unfortunately, the majority of this information is disseminated to administrators in workshops or graduate students majoring in educational leadership. However, as the pace of change in education accelerates and teachers are increasingly called to work together, the need for teachers to learn about communication tools also increases.

It is more likely that people will focus on actual problems instead of personal differences when they appreciate personality differences. In a widely distributed book on negotiation, Fisher and Ury (1981) urge us to focus on the problem, not the people. These authors counsel us to separate the people from the problem. It is hard to solve problems when we can't get beyond individual differences with other people. If you know how personality influences behavior and communication, you will be less likely to personalize differences and disagreements.

Together, Table 3.1 and Tables 3.2a and 3.2b make up a personality assessment that I have developed as a tool to help educators learn about themselves and others. It integrates foundational concepts of early personality psychology and ideas adapted from several resources that speak to the subjects of personality and communication (LaHaye, 1984; National Seminars Group, 2001; Wilson Learning Corporation, 1989).

Table 3.1 and Table 3.2a contain the directions. Turn first to Table 3.1 and go through each of the four columns, placing a checkmark on any word or phrase that describes you. For the assessment to be accurate, you must follow one very important rule: Go with your *initial reaction*. For example, if you read the phrase "Emotional Extremes" in Column 2 and at first believe that this accurately describes you, place a checkmark next to this characteristic. Some assessment takers may perceive themselves as being emotional but on reflection associate such a characteristic as a weakness and therefore not check the space. Check every characteristic that describes you, be it a perceived strength or weakness. Every column has characteristics that may be perceived as strengths or weaknesses, so the important thing is to check those characteristics that accurately describe you. The effectiveness of any psychometric test requires this level of honesty. After you have checked every word or phrase that describes you, add up the total checkmarks in each column.

Turn to Table 3.2a and complete the subtraction as described in Steps 1 and 2, plotting the results along their respective axes on the table; you should end up with only two dots. Now draw a line to

Table 3.1 Personality Assessment Checklist

Check any attribute that describes you in Columns 1, 2, 3, and 4. Total the checkmarks in each column.	
Column 1	*Column 2*
_ Decisive _ Factual _ Direct _ Strict, legalistic _ Like information _ Orderly _ Practical _ Cautious _ Uncommunicative _ Responsible _ Demanding _ Calculating _ Formal _ Goal oriented _ Industrious _ Economical _ Reserved _ Traditional	_ High energy _ Motivator _ Emotional extremes _ Impatient _ Active _ Charismatic _ Communicator _ Short attention span _ People oriented _ Opinionated _ Talk before I think _ Risk taker _ Loud _ Prefer quick pace _ Take charge _ Enthusiastic _ High need to control _ Competitive
Total	Total
Column 3	*Column 4*
_ Happy-go-lucky _ Noncommital _ Diplomatic _ Dependable when committed _ Carefree _ Untapped potential _ Impulsive _ Open _ Approachable _ Informal _ Easily influenced _ Undisciplined _ Congenial _ Easy to get to know _ Friendly _ Trusting _ Good with people _ Sociable	_ Prefer quiet environment _ Calm _ Hard time saying no _ Vulnerable, negative self-image _ Gentle _ Dependable _ Exact _ Simple dress _ Work well under pressure _ Supportive _ Deliberate actions _ Ask questions _ Good listener _ Soft spoken _ Risk averse _ Team oriented _ Devoted _ Permissive
Total	Total

Table 3.2a   Sample Assessment Graph

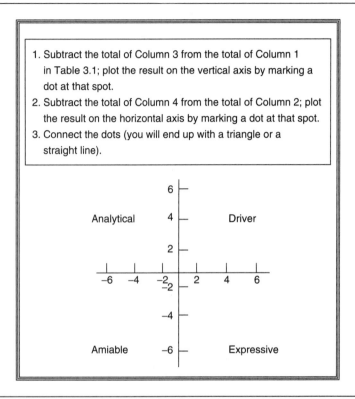

1. Subtract the total of Column 3 from the total of Column 1
   in Table 3.1; plot the result on the vertical axis by marking a
   dot at that spot.
2. Subtract the total of Column 4 from the total of Column 2; plot
   the result on the horizontal axis by marking a dot at that spot.
3. Connect the dots (you will end up with a triangle or a
   straight line).

that you simply formed a straight line. This will be the case if the result from either Step 1 or 2 was zero.

Table 3.2b is an example of a plot for a person who completed the personality assessment in Table 3.1 and Table 3.2a. This sample is included for illustration purposes only. The line that connects the two dots in Table 3.2b forms a triangle in the "Analytical" quadrant of the graph. It is likely that your triangle will be of a different size or location. If you ended up with a triangle of any size, then the quadrant in which your triangle resides contains the word that describes your personality type: Expressive, Driver, Amiable, or Analytical.

Table 3.2b Completed Assessment Graph

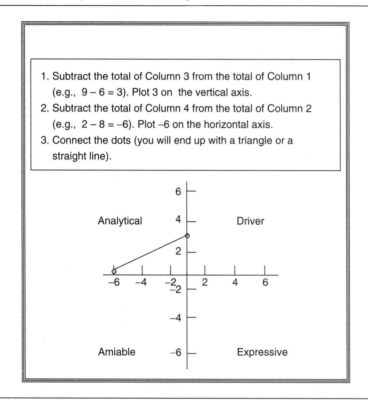

If your plot was a straight line rather than a triangle, look at the two personality quadrants that your line joins. The straight line means that the characteristics you exhibit, according to how you responded to the assessment, are evenly divided between these two personality types. The assessment is purposely designed to allow for the possibility that some people strongly exhibit characteristics of two personality types. Descriptions of the personality types are shown in Table 3.3.

The top of Table 3.3 lists commonly perceived strengths and weaknesses attributed to each personality type. These are described as "commonly perceived" because some of the listed weaknesses may actually be strengths, depending on the situation. For example, a listed weakness for the Analytical personality is that this person is a perfectionist. Perfectionists are slow to get things done because they are constantly looking for more information and want to be exact in their decisions. This may be a strength if a team of faculty

Table 3.3   Personality and Interaction

	Analytical	Expressive	Amiable	Driver
Strength	Thorough, calm, practical, high standards	Socially skilled, outgoing, persuasive	Team oriented, good listener, trusting, patient, helpful	Ambitious, goal oriented, dependable, organized
Weakness	Perfectionist, withdrawn, slow to get things done	Pushy, reactive, overbearing, manipulative	Hesitant, indecisive, vulnerable, too subjective	Stubborn, rigid, distant, critical
When Interacting				
Do	Be direct, provide evidence, be practical	Support brainstorms, discuss big picture, provide examples	Show sincere interest, be non-threatening, provide assurances	Show responsibility, control emotions, talk results, not personalities
Do not	Be disorganized, present half-baked ideas, be overassertive	Rush into business, debate, lack enthusiasm	Be cold or curt, be insensitive, be indecisive	Waste time visiting, try to build personal relationships

and staff is gathering information that is going to be used in a report to the state department of education. The more exact the report, the fewer questions later on.

As mentioned, the list of strengths and weaknesses in Table 3.3 provides a general sense of the common perceptions associated with each personality type. The strengths and weaknesses are more accurate for those teachers whose triangles in Table 3.2a are very large. If you ended up with a very small triangle or a straight line, the lists will be slightly less accurate. A small triangle indicates you more strongly exhibit characteristics of two or more personality types than a person who has a very large triangle. A large triangle indicates you strongly exhibit the characteristics described by your personality type. The fact is that everyone exhibits some characteristics of every personality type, but the strength of each characteristic associated with a given personality type varies for each individual.

There is a notable strength for those teachers who end up with a straight line or a very small triangle. Since these individuals more evenly exhibit characteristics from more than one personality type, they are usually able to effectively interact and communicate with a wide range of individuals. People with very large triangle plots are more likely to be viewed as extreme personalities and experience conflict with other people.

PERSONALITIES IN ACTION

Dan is a gentle man, quiet in manner but precise in action. He was a classroom elementary teacher for ten years before taking a position as a reading coordinator in his school. He is thorough in his work and ensures that teachers hold to the standards of the new reading program the school recently implemented. Most of the teachers work well with Dan, though some of them feel he could communicate a little more often and answer requests in a more timely manner. Dan gets along well with the school principal, but he sometimes feels the principal suggests ideas without having thought through their implications. This is disconcerting for Dan, because he likes to know that people offering suggestions aren't just "making things up" as they go. He has always liked to know the direct, practical implication of new ideas, and he wants people to walk the talk. Dan is an Analytical personality.

Sandra is an Expressive personality. She is an English teacher and works in a large, public high school. Sandra has been teaching for over twenty years, and her students see her as "cool" and fun. Sandra often organizes happy hour get-togethers with the other teachers and is not afraid to express her opinions. She recently worked on a committee to discuss the implications of inclusion in English and math courses. Inclusion, as defined by Sandra's school, meant that all students, including special education students, would be included in general education courses. Sandra found herself in the heat of many committee discussions, with some teachers perceiving her as trying to take over the conversation about how to effectively implement inclusion in the high school. Overall, Sandra is able to bring people together and lead a group, and she is now studying at the local university for her administrative license.

Eleanor works in a middle school that has recently transitioned from a junior high to a middle school. The middle school philosophy, as articulated by Eleanor's principal, embraces much of what Eleanor believes. Teachers are organized into interdisciplinary teams, and there is an emphasis on collaboration. Eleanor has always liked working in teams and in fact prefers it to working alone. She has never considered herself a spokesperson but takes pride in contributing to the team and helping others. Eleanor sees herself as able to put other people's needs above her own—this was actually the driving self-discovery that led her into teaching. Eleanor's friends say that people tend to take advantage of her because she does not know how to say "no." There is some truth to this assessment, as Eleanor has at times taken on too many assignments and duties because people recruited her or gave her additional tasks without really discussing it with her. Eleanor is best described as an Amiable personality.

Carlos is a high school history teacher and basketball coach. He is a stereotypical Driver personality. Carlos was a star player when he was in high school and graduated with honors from college. The principal in Carlos's high school regularly asks for his help with students who have been experiencing trouble in their studies and need structure. Carlos's businesslike approach in the classroom and on the basketball court has proven effective with problem students.

When Carlos first started coaching three years ago, the basketball teams were perennial losers, but under his guidance, the team now has a winning record and is probably a year away from state contention. Some parents have said that Carlos pushes students too hard and is critical of those who disagree with him. Carlos insists that his approach works. He spends little social time with other faculty and is not seen as the friendliest of teachers.

APPLYING THE CONCEPTS OF PERSONALITY TO YOUR SCHOOL

The major premise of personality theory is that people are different. Personality influences our actions, and our actions influence others. The framework that describes the four personality types offers a practical way to help teachers understand their own actions and those of their colleagues. Teachers can apply the tool of personality theory to their situations by answering questions specific to their schools.

Answer the three application questions that follow. The depth of thought you give to each question determines the level of application you perceive in each question. If you are working through this book with other teachers, answer these questions as a group.

1. Reflect on your experience as a teacher. What personality type do you have most difficulty with? Why?

2. Reflect on your experience as a teacher. What personality type do you get along best with? Why?

3. Does your ability to get along with a specific personality type depend on whether you are in a work setting or a social setting?

The three questions are useful for discussion without specifically naming individuals. The focus is on the personality type. Your answer to the questions also depends on your personality type, but there are some generalizations that tend to surface when a large number of people answer these questions. Tannen (1994), who has written extensively on relationships between men and women in the workplace, states that individuals do not always fit the general patterns of behavior that we might use to categorize them. However, there is value in identifying patterns and outlining generalizations. Generalizations help us organize our thoughts and make sense of the world, as long as we use caution in applying these generalizations and understand that there are exceptions.

The first prominent generalization that emerges from the three questions is that people have an easier time answering Question 2 than Question 1. Most people, regardless of their personality, generally agree that it is easy to get along with an Amiable person. This makes sense since Amiable people are good listeners. They are also team oriented and helpful. Amiable people tend to be genuinely interested in others, so they make friends very easily.

People do not generally agree as strongly on an answer for Question 1, but most people tend to experience difficulty with those personality types that demonstrate strong emotions or evoke those emotions in others. Expressive and Driver personalities tend to do this. Expressive personalities are themselves emotional. Expressive people may be talkative and loud if excited; they may be negatively vocal when offended. Drivers may be perceived as stubborn and critical, and this may hurt and offend others. People may form negative perceptions of Expressives or Drivers simply because they illicit strong emotions in others. Amiable and Analytical people do not tend to be as vocal, so people are not as quick to produce a strong judgment about them.

Effective communication between the various personality types is also influenced by situation: work or social. Analytical or Driver personalities may be very bothered by Expressive or Amiable faculty members who like to "visit" during planning periods. They may view this visiting as unnecessary socializing that cuts into the planning period. In a social setting, two Analytical personalities standing by the punch bowl at the holiday party may welcome an Expressive personality. The dynamics of any relationship is therefore influenced by the characteristics of the personalities and the situations in which those personalities interact.

CONCLUSION

We all have people with whom we get along and those we would rather avoid. You can think about your interactions with different people using the lens of personality theory to improve your relationships. The three application questions below will help you build productive relationships in your school. It is best to answer these three questions on your own rather than in a group.

Identify one person in your school with whom you have experienced conflict. Identify this person's personality.

How can you use the information in this chapter to improve your interaction with this person?

What is your administrator's personality? How can you use the information in this chapter to improve your interaction with your administrator?

Personality theory is not an exact science, nor can it solve every relationship problem. It is, however, a much-used tool across different disciplines and has helped people resolve conflict, improve teamwork, and generate understanding among and between colleagues. This knowledge put into practice can improve school collegiality.

CHAPTER FOUR

The Teacher's Role in Managing Conflict

Conflict occurs in every school for a variety of reasons. It may result because a school has initiated a new program or revamped its curriculum. Turnover among faculty and staff can lead to tensions between and among those who have just arrived and those who have been at the school for several years. Resources are often limited in public schools, and this too can be a great source of strain. People also have different beliefs and opinions, and this can lead to conflict. It may even result because of personality or cultural differences. Regardless of the causes, the consequences can be productive if managed properly. Teachers can help manage conflict and strengthen school collegiality in the process. Conflict in schools takes one of four forms, as shown in Table 4.1.

Conflict is usually characterized as a problem between two or more people, but it is also possible for an individual to feel it internally. Internal (or intrapersonal) conflict rarely remains confined to the individual experiencing it. Intrapersonal discord affects how we interact, speak, and behave around others and can easily lead to interpersonal problems.

One form of interpersonal conflict occurs between two people, as shown in Table 4.1. Two teachers may contend with each other for a variety of reasons. There may be disagreement about a particular student or competition over limited funds. Two teachers may just have difficulty getting along because of personality differences.

Table 4.1   The Four Forms of Conflict

Intrapersonal conflict	Occurs within a single person
Interpersonal conflict	Occurs between two people
Interpersonal conflict (intragroup)	Occurs among several individuals belonging to the same group
Interpersonal conflict (intergroup)	Occurs between two or more groups of people

But interpersonal conflict is not confined to two individuals. Hendricks (1991) identifies two additional types that are described in Table 4.1: *intragroup* and *intergroup* (p. 30). Intragroup conflict occurs between or among individuals belonging to the same group. An example of this would be communication problems among the math department faculty of a high school. Intergroup conflict occurs between groups—for instance, if the English department disagreed with the math department about how to implement inclusion in the school. Intragroup and intergroup conflicts still involve individuals, but group norms and values strongly influence the situation.

As a general rule, conflicts involving larger numbers of people are more difficult to resolve than those involving fewer people. Intergroup tensions in schools inevitably require administrative intervention. The most common type of conflict that faculty members experience is that between two people—teacher to teacher or teacher to administrator. Intragroup conflict among faculty is also common since today's teachers regularly work in groups and committees.

SOURCES OF CONFLICT

In a school setting, there are two common reasons why one of the forms of conflict might occur. The first is relational, the second is related to resources.

Relational Conflicts: Relational conflicts occur between individuals or groups and are caused by differences in personality, culture, values, beliefs, and opinions.

Resource Conflicts: Resource conflicts occur because there is not enough of something for every person or group, so the struggle to obtain it produces winners and losers. Schools, and especially public schools, are particularly susceptible.

Relational Conflict

Relationship problems often involve emotional displays and heated verbal exchanges. This is because it is difficult to separate the people from the problem (Fisher & Ury, 1981). For example, if two teachers have different opinions about bilingual education, it may be very difficult for them to separate the issue from how each personally views the other. The conflict may escalate if the two have different personality types.

A relational conflict can be intrapersonal or interpersonal. The following scenarios are examples of relational conflicts. Each example corresponds to one of the four forms of conflict shown in Table 4.1. After each scenario, in preparation for the next section on conflict resolution, ask yourself, "What can be done to resolve this conflict?" If you are working through this chapter with a group of faculty, read the cases and discuss them as a group.

Scenario 1

Intrapersonal Conflict: Elsie Crisp is a white female teaching at DeKalb County's Avondale High School in Georgia, where the student body is nearly 100 percent black. The school year 2002–2003 marked her sixth year at the school, and she has seen many white teachers leave for more affluent schools with predominately white students. While some teachers leave to move closer to home, Crisp says that many who leave are overwhelmed by the "culture shock" of all-black schools (Associated Press, 2003).

Those teachers who are leaving the minority-majority schools because of the culture shock to which Crisp refers are experiencing intrapersonal conflict. Most of these teachers probably want to contribute to the school, but they are not comfortable with the culture of the children in the school or do not understand how to work with people from different cultures. There is an inner struggle going on in these teachers. Some have resolved their dissonance by getting a job in a different school or leaving the profession.

Scenario 2

Interpersonal Conflict Between Two People: Mark has a hard time relating to his principal, Joyce. Joyce is very direct and curt in her communications with faculty, including being free with criticisms. Mark and Joyce have had several disagreements in Joyce's office and even some mild disagreements in faculty meetings. Mark feels like Joyce has little tact when communicating and believes that criticisms should not occur in faculty meetings but in private. Mark thinks Joyce is alienating her best faculty and creating uncomfortable situations. There has been some turnover in faculty the past two years, but many of the faculty who left did not contribute to the school in a manner that was consistent with the direction of the school's current improvement plan. Mark has ill feelings toward Joyce and feels he is at a decision point as to whether he should seek a transfer to another school within the district.

Scenario 3

Interpersonal Conflict Within a Group (Intragroup): Conway Elementary serves a large number of international students, many of whom do not speak English. A group of eight teachers has been asked to form a committee to discuss how the school can best meet the needs of these students. There is strong disagreement within the group as to whether the students should first attain literacy in their native languages or immediately receive as much instruction in English as possible. The committee's decision will have a major impact on curriculum, programs, and future faculty hires. The level of disagreement is so great that many in the group who previously had no trouble getting along are suddenly having problems with each other even outside the committee's work.

Scenario 4

Interpersonal Conflict Between Groups (Intergroup): Mayfield High School is organized by departments. The math department has its own culture, and teachers from that department tend to socialize together. The same is true of the art department. These two departments constantly seem to be at odds, and the individual teachers from the two departments almost always argue during faculty meetings. The principal feels that the arguments are distracting and counterproductive for everyone else involved in the meetings.

Resource Conflict

Resource conflict happens because there are always constraints on time, money, equipment, students, faculty, or facilities. It is difficult—sometimes even impossible—to provide a level of resources that would completely fulfill student and teacher needs. Teachers need resources to improve or complete their jobs, so conflict is sure to happen when there are not enough resources to go around. The people involved must take care to separate personal feelings from the resource problem. It is easy for teachers to mix personal feelings with their efforts to obtain basic resources because they are trying to help their students, classrooms, or programs.

The following scenarios are examples of resource conflicts. As before, each example corresponds to one of the four forms of conflict shown in Table 4.1. After each scenario, in preparation for the next section on conflict resolution, ask yourself, "What can be done to resolve this conflict?" If you are working through this chapter with a group of faculty, read the cases and discuss them as a group.

Scenario 1. Scarce Resource: Time

Intrapersonal Conflict: Kristen is a third grade teacher. She entered the teaching profession because she wanted to help young children. Kristen deeply believes that all children can learn, but now that she has been teaching for three years, she is struggling with how to allot her time in the classroom. She still holds onto the belief that all children can learn, but some of the children come from circumstances that make it very difficult to get them up to grade-level performance. In the class of twenty children, there are also those who are ready to move on to new material. When Kristen slows down and spends time with the children who are falling behind, the children who are ready to advance become bored and create behavioral distractions. Even with a teacher's aide, Kristen feels torn between spending extra time with those who are behind versus moving forward with those who are ready.

Scenario 2. Scarce Resource: Equipment

Interpersonal Conflict Between Two People: Brian's middle school has set out to increase student exposure to technology and its use. Raising funds to buy technology equipment has just gotten underway, so there are limited projectors, computers, and other technology-related equipment. The school has one new laptop that can hook up to a portable projector. Brian has been using the laptop and projector in his life science courses for the past four weeks. He plans to continue with this approach. The students are so excited that they have started finding demonstrations on the Internet, installing them on the laptop, and demonstrating them to the class. The problem is that that school's math teacher, Alma, also wants to integrate similar technology into her classroom. She feels that Brian has had enough time using the laptop and projector and others should have the opportunity. Brian doesn't want to give up the equipment now that the students are responding so well.

Scenario 3. Scarce Resource: Money

Interpersonal Conflict Within a Group (Intragroup): The district has allocated a one-time pool of money to Kearney High School. The money is only restricted in that it cannot be used for salaries and must be used for academic programs. The principal has called his administrative team together to determine whether the money should be channeled into existing programs or invested in equipment to start a technology lab. There is not enough money to do both, and the group is divided over how to use the money.

Scenario 4. Scarce Resource: Students

Interpersonal Conflict Between Groups (Intergroup): Tom and Elsie work in a public school district that allows open enrollment. A high school student in one area of town may enroll in a high school across town. There are three public high schools in the area. Tom is an English teacher and department head of the English department in his high school. He has been working hard to build the creative writing component of his department to attract students. Tom works regularly with his faculty, and as a team they brainstorm ideas about how to improve their program. The faculty in the department are very collegial and function as a unit. Tom feels fortunate to head such a department where everyone is willing to contribute. The team spirit that Tom has built enables him to spend a lot of time communicating with parents and "selling" them on the strength of the school's English department. Elsie works as the department head for the English department in another high school. She spends much of her time doing the same things as Tom, and she, too, has a very strong faculty. Tom and Elsie know each other and get along well, but at the same time, they share similar objectives while working for different schools in the same district. They both manage fine teams of faculty, but both groups are working to attract the same pool of students by strengthening their programs.

STRATEGIES TO RESOLVE CONFLICT

There are many reasons why conflicts may arise, and there are also several strategies to help resolve them. Every situation is unique, so the application of a strategy in one setting may not work in another. Teachers experiencing conflict should consider different strategies and use their judgment to apply the appropriate ones. The eight resolution strategies described in the following discussion agree with or add to the conflict resolution literature (Cox, 1993/2003) and are applicable to relational and resource conflicts in school settings.

1. Negotiation

The parties involved in the conflict engage in good-faith efforts to reach an agreeable solution. Negotiation involves give and take and requires that people honestly state their positions so that each party has as much relevant information about the other as possible. In negotiated solutions, people often feel that they have reached an acceptable agreement, though they may not have gotten everything they initially wanted. Negotiations that fully meet the needs of all parties involved are best described as collaborative or win-win.

2. Acquiring Additional Information

Acquiring additional information requires that the parties in conflict make a good-faith effort to do research, obtain materials, or talk to others. Additional information helps each party view the conflict from multiple perspectives. This strategy ensures that the parties in conflict are fully informed not only of each other's views but of the facts that surround the conflict.

3. Prioritizing According to School Goals

Defer to the priorities and goals of the school or organizational unit; doing so may determine the outcome of the conflict. This strategy assumes the school has some defined priorities and that teachers understand them.

4. Competition

The objective for each party is to win in competition. Each party should compete in the most ethical manner possible, but the result can still be described as win-lose since the two parties cannot both meet their goals. When resources are scarce, competition often results.

5. Employing Third-Party Intervention (Mediation)

Sometimes a conflict cannot be resolved by the parties involved in the conflict. An objective, credible third party intervenes to help them reach an agreement. The mediator must be credible with both parties for this strategy to be effective.

6. Introducing Training or Structured Interaction

A training intervention can increase knowledge or develop skills in a particular area, which could help resolve a conflict. Structured interactions allow individuals and groups to communicate in a formal, planned setting. A meeting with formal ground rules is an example of a format that leads to structured interactions.

7. Establishing a Policy

Established policies create guidelines for behavior and action. This strategy is very effective for problems and conflicts that tend to resurface.

8. Making Personnel Changes

Hire, fire, transfer or otherwise change faculty or administrators that are the subjects of the conflict. This is a last-resort strategy but may at times be necessary. Sometimes individuals transfer or leave on their own volition because they believe their ability to work with their current group of colleagues is limited.

Teachers can implement some resolution strategies on their own but not others. It is possible for teachers to implement the first four strategies without help from an administrator. For example, it is fairly easy to acquire additional information or engage in some sort of negotiation with another person if you are experiencing an interpersonal conflict. It is very difficult for teachers to implement the last four strategies without administrative involvement. Obviously, teachers cannot establish a policy for the entire school or initiate personnel changes, but they can provide input that influences decisions about training and policies. In addition, teachers are free to request transfers or to leave their jobs, so they do have some control over personnel changes.

MATCHING CONFLICTS TO STRATEGIES

As stated earlier, relational difficulties and resource constraints are the two most common sources of conflict in schools today. The scenarios from earlier in the chapter provide real-life examples from various school settings. It is likely that you have thought about the match between the strategies and the scenarios. Let's take that a step further.

Intrapersonal Conflict

In the first relational scenario, white teachers were experiencing intrapersonal conflict in all-black-student schools in Atlanta, Georgia. Many white teachers left for schools with a larger population of white children. Leaving is one resolution, and this is essentially the strategy of initiating a personnel change. In this case, the teachers do have control over their decision to stay or leave. Another possible strategy for these teachers is to receive training that helps them understand and operate in a culture that is different from their own. Such training may also provide strategies that help the teachers structure their classrooms in a way that produces an environment (structured interactions) that is more comfortable for both teacher and students. So for some, the answer is to leave and seek another environment; for others, training may be a strategy that leads a white teacher to a productive and fulfilling career in a school having mostly black students.

Kristen also had an intrapersonal conflict, but hers was caused by a constraint on her own time. This constraint stressed her ideal of helping every student equally, and she began to struggle with whether she should move on to additional material before every student was at a minimal competency level. First, Kristen should seek additional information. An effective way of doing that is to seek advice and mentoring from others who have confronted similar situations. Printed materials and research are also useful. Another option for Kristen is training. With the proper training, Kristen may learn about different classroom strategies whereby students help each other or learn in cooperative groups. There is no easy answer to Kristen's dilemma, but additional information and knowledge is a good place to start.

Interpersonal Conflict Between Two People

Mark was having trouble relating to his principal, Joyce. The source of the conflict had to do with differences in personalities. The starting point for Mark is to make sure not to take everything Joyce says too personally. Mark must control his personal reactions and feelings and examine the substance of Joyce's suggestions and comments. Are they aligned with what Mark believes to be the school's priorities (Strategy 3)? If Joyce has said nothing that differs from the priorities of the school but Mark still has difficulty with her, the next strategy would be to directly communicate with Joyce. This is the strategy of negotiation. If Mark has tried this and feels it is a dead end, there are still two more possibilities. Mark should seek training on personality interaction and communication skills. This is not an admission that the problem lies with Mark; rather, it is a proactive strategy for him to exhaust all possibilities before moving forward with the most drastic strategy, which is to leave and go to another school. Mark's departure would be classified as a personnel change.

Brian and Alma were not having a personality problem but a resource problem. In many districts, it is not uncommon for teachers to buy classroom supplies with their own money. Brian and Alma are in a difficult situation because neither teacher can afford to go out and buy a new laptop computer and projector. That investment could easily run to thousands of dollars. Brian and Alma should first try to negotiate and see if they can work out a schedule for using the equipment. They may even come up with a new idea that would solve the conflict, if successful, such as applying to a corporation for a school supply grant. If they cannot reach an immediate agreement, mediation (Strategy 5) is necessary. An administrator would have to be perceived as an impartial third party to resolve the conflict. It is common that conflicts over resources often result in the next strategy, that of designing a policy. In the case of the resource conflict between Brian and Alma, it may be necessary for an administrator to establish a policy that requires each person to check out the technology with the principal's office, stipulating that each person may keep the equipment for no more than two school days in a row.

Interpersonal Conflict Within a Group (Intragroup)

The two scenarios involving intragroup conflict are similar in that a group of teachers and administrators must make a decision. In the Conway scenario, the intragroup conflict is relational because the emotional involvement in the decision has been highly personalized. Members of the group feel passionately about either a bilingual program or one that emphasizes English. This level of passion has hurt relationships even after the committee meetings are over. The level of conflict in the Kearney High School scenario involves allocating resource either to existing programs or a new technology lab. This situation has not escalated to the same point as the Conway conflict and is best characterized as a resource conflict.

The primary strategy for the Conway group is to first consult school priorities, which may settle the argument. In El Paso, Texas, the Ysleta Independent School District has as one of its goals to produce students who can speak, read, and write in both English and Spanish at every grade level. Such a clearly pronounced goal might help settle the argument in this case. In another district, the context, history, and demographics may be different, and the school may not have such a goal. A concurrent strategy is to acquire as much information about each proposed program as possible. Schools regularly send out faculty and administrators to talk to other educators who have implemented programs similar to those they are considering. This information may be useful as the individuals and groups negotiate and search for a solution. If these strategies are unsuccessful, then administrative mediation is necessary.

Interpersonal Conflict Between Groups (Intergroup)

Conflict at the intergroup level usually requires administrative intervention. The intergroup conflict between the math and art departments at Mayfield High School in the fourth relational scenario becomes more serious if group differences turn into relational conflicts between individuals that belong to the groups. If this possibility looms, then the principal needs to consider two possible solutions: (1) look to create structured interactions whereby communication follows a formalized process, or (2) initiate personnel changes if the conflict becomes unmanageable.

The open enrollment problem is the one scenario in which the strategy of competition makes the most sense. Tom and Elsie each run a department but in different schools. Each department must compete to attract students. As long as each department competes ethically and honestly, competition is not necessarily a negative strategy. Tom has even said that the competition actually makes each department a little better.

Conflict Profiles

A large part of how individuals deal with a particular conflict is predicated on its nature. A teacher may have difficulty dealing with interpersonal clashes but calmly deal with resource dilemmas. Disposition and personality also influence how individuals resolve conflict. This is where conflict profiles can be useful: descriptions of how individuals tend to approach disagreement. A teacher's conflict profile may change over time, depending on situation, life stage, career, emotional maturity, and other variables that influence that teacher's thinking and behavior. It is also possible that a teacher exhibits a relatively consistent conflict profile over time, even as life events continue to influence perspectives and beliefs.

Rate yourself according to your first reaction to the profile descriptions that follow. Each profile describes a different way that people handle conflict with others. The descriptions are not intended to be good or bad. There are strengths and weaknesses associated with each profile type, so there is no one right answer. It is possible to rank different profiles equally. Rate the extent to which each profile accurately describes you, according to the following scale:

5 = Very strongly describes me

4 = Describes me

3 = Somewhat describes me

2 = Vaguely describes me

1 = Doesn't describe me

Profile 1

I am not shy about confronting disagreement. I am direct and let people know what I think. For example, I have no problem letting the waiter know if my food is not to my liking. My emotions sometimes get the best of me, but I am usually willing to stand by my convictions, even if I have said something I wish I could take back. I am competitive, and I don't like to lose.

Rating: 5   4   3   2   1

Profile 2

I believe that conflict can be productive. It is necessary to reach middle ground, and it helps to balance out extreme thinking and extreme positions. People should be allowed to voice their opinions, but objections to those opinions should be freely heard. Usually, an agreement is the result of give and take. Negotiation and compromise is the best way to resolve conflict.

Rating: 5   4   3   2   1

Profile 3

I do not believe resolution has to necessarily be a win-lose process. An effective resolution can meet everyone's needs. It is important to explore points of agreement and disagreement, because new alternatives can result. Everyone can win if we put our heads together.

Rating: 5   4   3   2   1

Profile 4

I like to let people know that I support them. It is more effective to find points of agreement than points of disagreement. Points of disagreement often lead to more disagreement, eventually degenerating into personal attacks and negative feelings. I don't like when people get hurt or upset, and I am willing to help do whatever is possible to keep the peace. An effective way to resolve conflict is to get beyond your own needs and think about it from the other person's perspective.

Rating: 5   4   3   2   1

Profile 5

I am very cautious about becoming involved in any conflict. It is too easy to add fuel to the fire. Sometimes it is best to stay on the sidelines and let things work themselves out. I believe that my actions speak louder than words, so I usually don't feel the need to speak up or immediately make my opinions known.

Rating: 5   4   3   2   1

The profile descriptions that you ranked the highest most represent how you attempt to resolve problems with others. Each conflict profile is now explained in more detail:

Profile 1: Competitor

The competitor often displays dominant characteristics during conflict, as indicated by the profile description. Some have characterized competitors as aggressive people who have a "win-lose" attitude and primarily think of their own needs but not the needs of others. While this may be true, this approach to conflict can be effective when competing for resources and was an appropriate strategy for Tom's and Elsie's departments in the resource conflict Scenario 4.

A competitive posture is less effective when the resource conflict is between two people who work for the same school or deal with each other on a regular basis; competition may foster ill will between the two parties. Conversely, if you are competing for something against people you do not know, a competitive approach may be quite appropriate. An example of this would be competing for a grant for your classroom or school.

Profile 2: Negotiator

The negotiator is also known as the *compromiser*. This is the teacher who believes that everyone must give up a little to get a little. Negotiators are often described as those who want to meet their needs, but they realize that other people want their needs met as well. The problem is that everyone's needs cannot be fully met, because there is only so much to go around. If there is only one piece of pie and you eat it, there is no more pie left; therefore, the best solution is to share it, even though neither of us will be fully satisfied.

This approach is effective when there is no possibility of expanding the pie. Negotiators have been referred to as realists, because they understand that there are multiple needs and that life is often a game of give and take. A negotiator would not be opposed to a mediator who can help divide the pie in the most equitable manner possible. In the resource conflict Scenario 2, Brian and Mary cannot both use the laptop and projector all the time, so the strategy of negotiation provides a starting point to resolve the conflict.

Profile 3: Collaborator

The collaborator does not believe in the disappearing pie. This is the positive teacher or administrator who believes that through teamwork and effort, it is possible to bake more pie rather than be satisfied with the existing one. The collaborator has been referred to as an idealist, because the underlying belief is that everyone's needs can be met. If people brainstorm and create solutions, there is no reason to give up anything.

The collaborator is frequently viewed as the best conflict profile because of the win-win mentality that accompanies it. The collaborator is effective in situations where creativity and teamwork are needed if solutions to problems are unknown. In cases where new solutions aren't likely to be realistic or there are resource limitations, the negotiator may be more effective than the collaborator. For example, if it is clear that a teacher and administrator cannot get along, there may not be a win-win solution. It may be necessary for the teacher to transfer to another school because the history of conflict may be irreconcilable.

In the relational conflict Scenario 2, Mark has trouble communicating with his principal, Joyce. If Mark is able to sit down with Joyce and work through their communication difficulties, he may be able to stay at his school and be productive. Joyce, in turn, would retain a valued employee and have someone who can testify to her willingness to work through problems. This would produce a win-win solution.

Profile 4: Pleaser

Pleasers are those teachers who are willing to accommodate the needs of others above their own because this leads to agreement. Agreement, in the pleasers' eyes, is their primary goal, and they see little reason to fight or disagree. Pleasers are giving, team-oriented people, but they are not good decision makers. They can help smooth things over during intense conflict. They desire fairness, and they do not want to see anyone lose, though, ironically, they are willing to sacrifice their own self-interests.

Profile 5: Avoider

The avoider has been contrasted psychologically with the competitor. The competitor is dubbed as adopting a strategy of "fight" and an avoider a strategy of "flight." Avoiders flee from conflict because they do not like it, they do not know how to handle it, or they simply do not consider the issue worth arguing about. In the resource conflict Scenario 3, the teachers at Kearney who want the technology lab may realize that realistically, there is no chance of using the money that way. One possibility is for these teachers to walk away from the discussions since they see little hope. When the issue is not worth fighting over or there is no prospect for victory or mutual gain, the time to walk away may be at hand.

The idea of avoiding conflict can be an effective short-term strategy when emotions are high and clouding sensible judgments about reaching resolution. Thomas Jefferson was said to have counseled this: If angry, take 10 seconds, if very, very angry, take 100. Time away from a conflict often leads to the path of resolution. Avoidance is usually not effective in the long term since the root of a conflict seldom disappears on its own.

CONCLUSION

Conflict is a reality in every school. The question is not if conflict will happen, but how you will handle it. Teachers who appropriately handle conflict contribute to a school environment that productively deals with disagreement. This increases school collegiality and very likely can help retain good teachers that may otherwise choose to leave the profession.

Teachers cannot afford to believe that administrators can solve every problem in their schools. As demonstrated, there are different strategies for dealing with different types of conflict, and your knowledge of resolution strategies serves as an important guide for resolving conflict. Different conflict profile types will be more effective in different conflict scenarios, meaning no single conflict profile is effective in every situation. Your conflict profile indicates how you tend to approach conflict, but your results on the assessment do not prevent you from drawing on the strengths of other profiles in particular situations. The four questions that follow are application oriented. These questions will help you apply the contents of the chapter to a specific situation. The questions will also help you draw on the various qualities from the different profiles if they are effective means for resolving the conflict you identify.

List one conflict you currently confront in your school environment. Is it a relational or a resource conflict?

Is your conflict profile description an asset or a liability when dealing with this particular conflict?

What qualities from the other conflict profiles might you apply to help resolve the conflict?

What are some strategies, as explained in the chapter, that you might use to help resolve the conflict?

CHAPTER FIVE

The Growing Need for Teamwork

Preteen students have historically been classified as junior high students, but schools across the country are currently adopting the name and philosophy of what is known as the middle school. The philosophy of the middle school concept is synonymous with teamwork. It encourages collaboration and organizes teachers into interdisciplinary teams with common planning periods. In some middle schools, even the physical arrangements aim to maximize teacher-to-teacher interactions. Teachers belonging to the same team have adjacent work spaces to create opportunities for collaboration. This middle school philosophy contrasts with traditional arrangements whereby teachers are organized by department with little or no effort to coordinate planning periods.

The growing interaction between and among teachers is not confined to middle school teachers. Teachers today, whether at the elementary, middle, or high school level can expect to participate in committees or workgroups throughout their careers. The classroom responsibilities that accompany a teaching career have not gone away, it is just that today's expectations include working in teams. The need for teamwork may be driven by the goals of the principal or directives from the state department of education. Effective teamwork among teachers can be the difference between school success or failure. Rob Weil, deputy director of educational issues for the American Federation of Teachers, recently said, "In other countries there's a belief: Teachers working together to really polish their craft is really important to the quality of education" (Associated Press, 2002b).

Teamwork does not happen automatically. The interactions among team members are complex and dynamic. There is potential for confusion and misinterpretation as teachers of different personalities, experience, and skill try to work toward common objectives. Teachers can work more effectively with others in team settings by learning why teams are important and how they work.

WHAT IS A TEAM?

In the early part of the twentieth century, the focus of work life was squarely on pushing employees to complete their jobs at all costs. There was little regard for feelings, attitudes, and interactions among employees. By the middle of the century, the human side of work life began to emerge as researchers such as Abraham Maslow (1943/2000) and Douglas McGregor (1957) called attention to the psychological and social needs of people in the workplace. The interest in teams soon followed and is today a vast and important field of study. The promise of effective teams is that the two or more people working together are more effective than each person working separately.

A team is composed of a group of people, two or more, who are working toward a common purpose. The strength of a team lies in the different knowledge, skills, and abilities of the people who make it up. In true teams, individuals work *interdependently*. This means that team members rely on each other to accomplish work—each helps or complements the others. In earlier times, the term *team* was applied to any group of people working for the same administrator, even if each person worked independently. There is a big difference between working interdependently and working independently. People who work independently usually do not know or care what their colleagues do. They rely on an administrator to manage the big picture and coordinate each of the individual tasks. People who work interdependently want their colleagues to be successful because the actions of one person affect the jobs of others.

In education, it is increasingly difficult to keep or adopt the independent mindset. This is because student preparation at one level affects success at another. The sequence of course and subject progression means that one teacher's effectiveness influences another's. For example, if a group of students takes fourth grade mathematics with one teacher but is not adequately prepared for fifth grade mathematics with another teacher, then problems will arise both for the students and between the two teachers. The fourth grade teacher may feel the students are adequately prepared for fifth grade mathematics but that the fifth grade teacher's expectations are too high and the teaching style inappropriate for fifth graders. The fifth grade teacher is upset, believing that the fourth grade teacher did not prepare last year's students for this year's curriculum. If the teachers team together to discuss expectations and teaching methodology, the potential for professional growth and student success is greater than if the teachers do not communicate and are unaware of each other's perspective. Today, teachers regularly work on teams to discuss issues of curriculum, teaching methodology, sequencing, and other school issues.

Teams in schools are sometimes formed to solve problems or implement changes. Schools will continue to rely on effective teams to implement changes in the face of the 2001 No Child Left Behind Act (NCLB). This new law and revision of the Elementary and Secondary Education Act represents systematic reforms in elementary and secondary education in the United States. The four major areas of change include allowing for parental controls, implementing best practices based on research, increasing accountability, and expanding local control and flexibility (U.S. Department of Education, 2003). States across the nation have already implemented various accountability measures in efforts to ensure that their schools meet the requirements of the legislation. Schools that fall short find themselves on probation or watch lists, and they must make changes to stay in good standing with their state departments of education. The success of any school, whether it is striving to meet the requirements of NCLB or some other goal, rests on the ability of the teachers to work with other teachers, administrators, parents, and students.

Any time a group of teachers is brought together to work in a team, there is great potential to achieve positive results. On the other hand, there is also potential for damaged relationships, disagreements, and miscommunication. That is why it is important to know how teams work and the stages they go through in making changes or solving problems.

EFFECTIVE TEAMS

The best way to learn about teams is to do an exercise that requires you to work in one. If you are working through *Teachers Working Together for School Success* with a group, do the following exercise together. If you are reading this book on your own, try to find two other people to do the exercise with you. Even if you are reading the book alone, you will be able to see how the exercise leads to an important discussion of teams. The exercise takes less than five minutes.

Learning Activity Instructions for the Triangle Challenge

Form teams of three people. Team members cannot talk to each other before or during the exercise. You will also need to have several blank sheets of paper and a pencil for each team member. The task is to make as many triangles as possible in 60 seconds. Every person on the team must make one side of every triangle, otherwise the triangle does not count toward your final score. Begin the exercise, timing the team. When the 60 seconds have elapsed, have the team count the number of triangles that were completed according to the instructions.

Allow the teams to talk about their results for two minutes. Have the teams discuss how they could improve their score if they did the exercise all over again. Repeat the exercise as described and have the teams count their triangles from the second iteration of the exercise.

Have the teams compare their results from the two trials. Did the team improve? Why or why not? What factors affected the results?

There are three possible results from the Triangle Challenge. First, many teams improve their score the second time. A second possibility is that a team's score did not improve and actually went down. Third, it is possible that the team's score stayed the same.

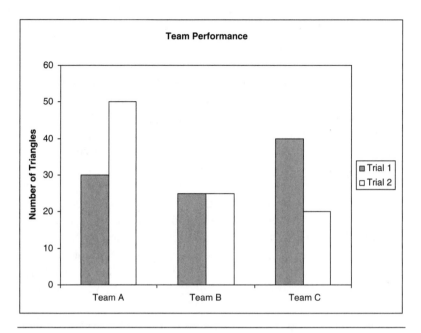

Figure 5.1 Differences in Team Performance

Figure 5.1 displays the possible outcomes for a team's performance on the Triangle Challenge.

The Triangle Challenge is a straightforward exercise, and when a large group does the exercise, it is very typical that the majority of teams show improvement from Trial 1 to Trial 2. If the group is large enough, there are usually a few teams whose results resemble Team B's or Team C's in Figure 5.1. Teams that improve their scores typically attribute their success to communication. Between the first and second trials, the team members were able to figure out a better strategy to improve their score. But it is possible that some teams communicated and still did not improve their scores. What is it about a team and how the individuals of the team work together that leads to a particular result? What affects teamwork?

The key to effective teams lies with the effort of each team member. Teams that improve over time (1) understand the objective, (2) go through four stages that lead to productive outcomes, and (3) are composed of a mix of people who were able to work together. Let's look at these more closely.

Team Objective

The making of a successful team starts when the team members understand the objective and agree with it. Although this point seems obvious, the importance lies with the difference between understanding and agreement. Understanding means that the team members internalize the true purpose of the objective, but that doesn't mean that they necessarily believe that it is worth pursuing. To gain understanding, faculty must dialogue. In a dialogue, people observe the thinking of others, but they also become observers of their own thinking (Senge, 1990, p. 242). Agreement means that team members believe the objective is worth pursuing because they believe the benefits of meeting the objectives outweigh the costs. For example, if the faculty is required to attend two training sessions as a team to learn about the different learning styles of students, the team can implement what it has learned if everyone understands the philosophy of learning styles and agrees that it can be applied in the school.

The objective in the Triangle Challenge is easy to understand. Since the task is easy to understand and there is not much controversy in drawing triangles, it is easy to reach agreement. Teachers sometimes encounter difficulty understanding or agreeing with the team objective if it is controversial. Usually, agreement is the sticking point. For instance, curriculum changes tend to generate controversy because teachers may not agree with the changes they are being asked to make.

In some cases, it is difficult to understand the objective because there is no clear definition of it. If the objective is not easily understood, then it will be difficult to gain understanding or agreement on it. In one high school, the English department was asked to be the pilot to implement inclusion in the classroom. Each of the teachers had a different definition of what they thought inclusion meant and the responsibilities that went along with it. Thus, when the department faculty discussed inclusion, there was a lot of confusion. The department never really arrived at one definition of inclusion. There was a lot of frustration, since the English faculty was eventually supposed to explain to other departments how to properly implement inclusion in their classrooms.

The best way for each team member to formulate an opinion about the objective is to first try to understand it. Once members understand the objective, they are in a better position to assess whether they agree with it. Understanding starts by gathering information, including reading existing documents related to the objective and, most important, asking administrators and other teachers how they understand it. This process itself may lead to a common understanding or definition of the objective.

Team Stages

Though simple, the Triangle Challenge powerfully demonstrates the stages of teamwork. Dr. Min Basadur (1995) confirmed that teams go through four stages when solving problems. Dr. Basadur has done research on teams in various settings and discovered that effective teams (1) generate ideas, (2) conceptualize those ideas into solutions, (3) optimize to find the most effective solution, and (4) implement the solution. Popular author Roger von Oech (1986), in a more light-hearted manner, identifies four stages of creativity: (1) the explorer looks for new ideas, (2) the artist puts the ideas together, (3) the judge decides which idea is best, and (4) the warrior puts the idea to work.

As mentioned earlier, teams that show drastic improvement from Trial 1 to Trial 2 in the Triangle Challenge have typically engaged in animated discussion during the discussion period. Effective teams accomplish their goals in the four sequential stages and the Triangle Challenge leads most teams naturally through them. I call them *brainstorming, experimenting-analyzing, evaluating,* and *implementing* (these are shown in Figure 5.2).

The first stage of teamwork requires *brainstorming* about *how* to complete the objective, where each team member offers ideas about how the score can be improved. *Experimenting and analyzing* means that teams discuss, scrutinize, and compare possible solutions. The *evaluation* stage is when the team must decide on one strategy from the various possibilities, because the constraints of time and resources always lead to the last stage, *implementation.*

All four stages of teamwork are evident in the Triangle Challenge. Teams that achieve impressive results brainstorm between one trial and the next. This must take place quickly because there are only two minutes before the team must begin drawing triangles again.

In the second stage, team members *experiment* with the different ideas. Team members can often be seen drawing triangles in new

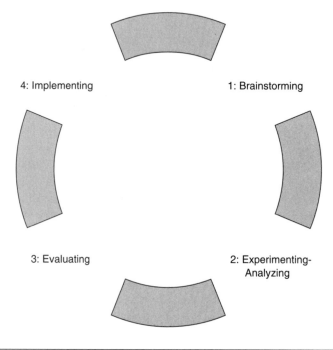

4: Implementing   1: Brainstorming

3: Evaluating   2: Experimenting-
                                      Analyzing

Figure 5.2   Team Stages

ways or positioning themselves around the table differently as they experiment with the ideas that emerged from the brainstorming.

As the two minutes draw to a close, the team must decide on one strategy. It may be that each person offered a different idea, but the team must *evaluate* which idea is most likely to produce the most triangles. The best strategy may be one team member's original idea but most often, it is a combination of ideas synthesized into one solution that produces the final strategy. The different ideas from the brainstorming stage can come together in a coherent solution when people go through the experiment stage. The evaluation stage is completed when the team members have agreed on the final strategy. *Implementation* occurs when the two-minute discussion period ends and the team actually begins drawing triangles again.

The second stage of experimenting-analyzing requires additional commentary. It is not always possible to experiment with the different ideas from the brainstorming stage, as it is in the Triangle

Challenge. A high school suspension committee may be called on to evaluate long-term suspensions and make recommendations to school policy that might decrease the need for suspension. It is not realistically possible to experiment before the group makes a policy recommendation to the principal. In this case, it is only possible to analyze all and any information related to solutions that have been used in other schools or that are documented in educational resources. This analysis will eventually help the committee evaluate the solution that they think will be most effective. Teachers and administrators sometimes travel to schools that have implemented a change that is similar to one they are considering, or they look for research related to the proposed change. These are strategies of observation and analysis and fulfill the second stage of teamwork when experimentation is not possible.

The work of many teams is continuous. This means that once the team implements a change, it goes on to evaluate whether the change is producing the intended outcomes. If it is not, then adjustments must be made, and these will be most effective if the team again goes through the four states.

Teams that go through the four stages of teamwork are effective because they draw on the input of each team member and use that input to decide what is best for the team. The four stages offer a natural, sequential prescription that allows a team to improve its performance or solve a given problem. A team will not be as effective as it could be if it skips one of the stages, even if there are pressures that require immediate decisions. For example, at Booker T. Washington Elementary, the principal was under tremendous pressure to make broad, sweeping changes when his school was put on probationary status by the New Mexico State Department of Education (Tallman, 2002). There was little or no time for the teachers to brainstorm in their grade level meetings about changes to help the school. This meant that the first three stages of teamwork were skipped and implementation started immediately, a situation that should be avoided if at all possible. It is infinitely better to spend even a limited amount of time on brainstorming, experimenting-analyzing, and evaluating than no time at all. Sometimes decisions do have to be made quickly, but if the team is not asked for any input and asked to jump to implementation immediately, problems are sure to surface along the way. Emergencies often place teachers and administrators in difficult situations where hasty decisions have to be made without the benefit of team input. The question is whether the emergency could have been avoided in the first place by using the power of teams.

Team Members

A team is composed of two or more people, but the optimal team ranges from three to six people. Hackman and Oldman (1980/2000) indicate that the composition of the team is an important determinant of team success. The composition has to do with the range of skills, abilities, and personalities as well as the number of members. The mix influences how effectively the team completes each of the team stages or whether it even goes through each stage.

There are several guidelines that teachers and administrators can follow to improve teamwork. First, it is very important to have a diverse team if the team is trying to solve a difficult problem or make a recommendation that requires substantial work. The team needs experienced teachers and new teachers, and teachers who are outspoken and those who are methodical and cautious. When the composition of the team is diverse, the likelihood of achieving innovative and effective results increases substantially.

It is also important to have a diversity of personalities on the team. Certain personalities tend to excel at different stages of teamwork, and teams are more effective if they can work through all four stages. Table 5.1 describes the type of skill that is necessary to complete each stage of teamwork and the personality type that, in general, exhibits characteristics that match that stage.

Expressive personalities are socially skilled and unafraid to offer new ideas. This is important in the brainstorming stage. As mentioned in Chapter 3, Table 3.4, one way to encourage Expressive people is to support brainstorming and allow them to discuss broad ideas. But the Expressive personality type is not the most effective at experimentation or analysis. Experimentation and analysis requires people who are thorough and exacting, who can put ideas to the test. The Analytical personality is fit for such a task and can add great value to the experimenting-analyzing team stage. The Analytical personality is usually detail oriented and can probably figure the costs and benefits of each alternative that came out of the brainstorming stage. These skills are also valuable in the evaluation stage. Drivers also play a role in this stage because of their ability to organize and move toward action. Drivers' ambitious nature and

Table 5.1   Personality and Team Stages

Team Stage	Required Skill or Ability	Personality Match
Brainstorming	Creativity, generating new ideas	Expressive
Experimenting-Analyzing	Testing, researching	Analytical
Evaluating	Ability to compare alternatives	Analytical and Driver
Implementing	Moving to action; getting things done	Driver

desire for action means that they can move the rest of the team to stage four, the implementing stage.

Noticeably absent from Table 5.1 is the Amiable personality. And yet, to function properly, teams need a person with an Amiable personality. The Amiable person listens well and is generally team oriented, trusting, patient, and helpful, attributes that carry a team forward through each of the stages of teamwork. The Amiable person is the glue that holds the team together.

The ideal team, then, should contain all four different personalities. This is especially true when the team is charged with investigating or solving new problems. A team with only Expressive personalities may not get past the brainstorm stage. The team would probably generate several different ideas but have difficulty completing a task without the other personalities. Similarly, a team of Drivers may be so eager to begin doing something—anything—that the first stages crucial to problem solving are completely ignored. In Figure 5.1, Teams B and C did not improve. Team C's performance actually decreased. In real team situations, this sometimes happens if the people on the team have similar personalities and skills when the task at hand calls for team diversity.

It is possible that certain team efforts may be completed without all four personality types, depending on the job the team is asked to complete. For example, scheduling teacher duty may be a source of contention. If a teacher from each grade level is asked to work in a team to make recommendations to improve the equity of the schedule, there would be an emphasis on brainstorming. The team's role, in this case, is advisory in nature. A Driver may get frustrated on such a team since the recommendations may or may not be implemented. Conversely, suppose the Internet has proven an effective teaching tool in a middle school life-science class. If the school has obtained grant funds to buy additional laptops and projectors, a team of knowledgeable teachers may have to spearhead the effort to equip additional classrooms. In this case, the decision has already been made to "wire" the additional classrooms. The implementation team might well consist of teachers who are valued for their analytical knowledge (Analyticals) and know how to implement a project to completion (Drivers).

People with different personalities, skills, and abilities have various strengths at each stage of teamwork. It is important that the talents and personalities of the team members match the task at hand.

Team Size

A final factor important to team effectiveness is that of team size. In a groundbreaking book on how individuals function in teams, Olson (1965) outlined the importance of team size, the actual number of people who are on the team. Olson found that the size of a team influences the behavior of the individual members. When the team is small, say only four members, the unspoken pressure to contribute to the team is quite high. It will be obvious in a small group if someone is not pulling his or her weight. In Olson's parlance, "social incentives" are effective in small groups, but their effectiveness decreases as the size of the group increases. It is easier to assume someone else will do the work if the team is large because it is easier to blend in and hide from responsibility. Hackman and Oldman (1980/2000) warn that danger is near if the team is overstaffed.

In a large group, there are so many different ideas that it is unlikely that the group will reach agreement on a plan of action. In addition, the more reserved faculty members are not likely to offer their input in such a setting. This means that the knowledge of the group is not fully tapped.

There is a strategy that can help overcome the risks associated with large teams: Break it up into smaller groups. Depending on the objective, each smaller group may work on a different part of the problem or each may work on the entire scope and compare results. It may be very productive to have different teams working on the same problem if the school is hoping to compare different ideas.

Most teachers have had the experience of attending a large school meeting because the administrator wants to solicit faculty input to solve a problem. The intent is admirable, but this manner of obtaining the input is not effective. These sessions inevitably lead to disagreements and complaints that have nothing to do with the issue at hand and notable silence from voices that may have good ideas. Problem solving is more effective in smaller teams. Grade level or department meetings are examples of settings that are conducive to problem solving.

Large faculty and staff meetings are appropriate to give information and, to some extent, hear concerns. The issue of school violence received heightened attention after the Columbine shootings in Colorado. In this case, a large group meeting in the school cafeteria was an appropriate forum to hear concerns and address questions. Such sessions took place in schools around the country after the shootings and surely helped ease faculty anxiety, but new ideas about handling or reducing school violence are best generated through the work of smaller faculty teams.

CONCLUSION

Teachers who work in teams must be willing to learn together. Senge (1990) points out that team learning takes practice. Imagine trying to build a great theater ensemble or championship sports team without practice (p. 238). Faculty must be willing to learn with and about each other to create effective teams. This is especially important in education since it is not always possible to implement the ideal theories of teams by matching personalities with the task. More often than not, in education, resources are limited, and the available person— the one who is volunteered or whose turn comes up—must serve on a team. Individual teachers who have knowledge of teams and how they work can improve the effectiveness of any team they are part of. The checklist that follows is a guide to help teachers work in teams, whatever the objective and whoever the team members.

Checklist: Individual Effectiveness in Team Performance

1. Know your individual strengths and weaknesses.

2. Match your individual knowledge, skills, and abilities to those tasks you think you are best able to perform.

3. Realize that every team member has strengths as well as weaknesses.

4. Allow the team time to work through the stages of teamwork; be patient with yourself and others.

5. Ask for the training you feel you need to be successful.

6. Use conflict resolution skills to work toward solutions (see Chapter 4).

7. Use the information in Chapter 2 to identify the different personalities on the team and how you work with them.

Several items on the checklist emphasize how essential productive relationships are to teamwork. It is also important that every team understand the objective it is working toward. There should be some level of agreement about the value of the objective as well. Last, all members' contributions to the team will be strengthened if they know the stages of teamwork and the impact of personalities and group size on team functioning. Ultimately, each teacher's contribution to the team starts with the first item on the checklist—and that is because the essence of teamwork requires that all members examine themselves before they examine others.

CHAPTER SIX

Working With Your Administrator

T eachers interact with some school administrators on a daily basis and rarely see others. The focus of this chapter is to help teachers work with those administrators who directly lead or share responsibility for leading a school. The titles of these school administrators range from principals and deans to assistant principals and coordinators. Central administrators, such as superintendents and associate superintendents, have less daily contact with school faculty and are not the subject of this chapter. In addition, Buckingham and Coffman's (1999, p. 33) twenty-five years of research with The Gallup Organization found that, more often than not, employees leave their immediate managers and administrators, not their jobs. This means that teachers who leave their schools or the teaching profession often leave because of bad experiences with school-level administrators. A successful relationship between a teacher and an administrator depends on both people, so it is important for teachers to know a bit about working with administrators who have different leadership styles.

Teachers who have worked under different principals know that administrators have different leadership styles, which means they have different ways of communicating and accomplishing their objectives. Faculty, staff, and even students formulate perceptions about school administrators based on their leadership styles.

Administrators take graduate coursework or attend training sessions to learn about their leadership styles. This training is valuable because it helps them understand their strengths and weaknesses and how to more effectively work with faculty. While leadership training for administrators is widely available, little effort has been extended to help faculty learn about this area. Faculty training in this area is important for two reasons. First, faculty who understand different leadership styles have a better foundation from which to work with different administrators. Second, the knowledge that faculty gain by learning about leadership styles is invaluable for those who will one day become administrators themselves.

ADMINISTRATIVE LEADERSHIP STYLES

Tom has been a high school math teacher for eight years. Teaching is actually Tom's second career. He retired from the army and decided that he wanted to spend the rest of his professional life teaching high school mathematics. When Tom left the army, he thought he had left behind strict, by-the-book leadership that was squarely focused on the task at hand. He was looking forward to working in an organization with a more humanistic approach to management. As things turned out, Tom's first principal, Mrs. Johnson, was not that much different from his last commanding officer. Mrs. Johnson was very businesslike and always got straight to the point. All of the other teachers warned Tom that she didn't like to hear about anyone's personal life because she thought they would eventually use that information as an excuse when they had to miss work or a committee assignment. Tom was used to a rigid leadership style from his army days, so he was able to work well under Mrs. Johnson even though he had been looking forward to a different leadership approach. Many of Tom's colleagues felt that it was difficult to work with her. There were communication problems between certain faculty members and Mrs. Johnson. People got things done, but faculty and staff seemed to be afraid to make mistakes or offer suggestions. Mrs. Johnson eventually took a job in central administration because her achievements at the high school, as measured by the state, were impressive.

The replacement principal had a very different leadership style from his predecessor. Mr. White was friendly and easygoing. He called a staff meeting the first day the faculty returned from summer vacation and said that his first goal was to get to know every faculty member and sit down with each and every person to discuss ideas, concerns, and perceptions about the school. Mr. White followed through with his goal, and because of his ongoing efforts to build relationships and include people in decision making, he is well liked by the faculty. Strangely, after two years, the school's overall performance has declined, and there is a sense that administration is a bit disorganized.

Tom's experience is not that unusual. Some administrators are very task focused, and they are able to set goals for the school and achieve them. Other administrators are very focused on meeting the needs of faculty. Administrators who are not personable with faculty often experience communication problems with their employees, much like Mrs. Johnson. On the other hand, administrators who focus on goals seem to produce excellent results. Administrators like Mr. White are popular with faculty but are sometimes criticized for not making necessary, tough decisions because they are afraid to hurt anyone's feelings. Not all administrators fall into one of these two extreme leadership styles. Many fall somewhere between the people-centered approach of Mr. White and the focused, businesslike approach of Mrs. Johnson.

The research on leadership styles is extensive, and early studies have had a lasting influence and are strongly reflected in current theory and modern training modules. Writers continue to examine leadership styles from different perspectives and look for novel approaches to help practitioners, but two elements of leadership found in past studies (Blake & Mouton, 1964; Blanchard, 1985; Stogdill, 1948) are still applicable today: Leaders can be described as *people centered* or *work centered*. These descriptions align with the dimensions described by previous research but are simple and self-explanatory.

A principal who is work centered is concerned about results and focuses on policies, rules, and the organization of the school. Results come about because of structure and the emphasis on tasks. Such principals are not focused on managing the relationships among faculty who are on a committee, but they ensure that each committee understands what it is supposed to accomplish. An administrator at the opposite extreme is very people centered and sensitive to teacher input. This type of leader is also able to motivate people and manage relationships between and among team members. An administrator who is work centered can exhibit characteristics of a people centered leader, and the reverse is also true. Tom's principals represented two extremes, but many administrators do exhibit some attributes that emphasize work and others that emphasize people.

Some leadership theories (e.g., Fiedler & Chemers, 1974) suggest that different situations call for different types of leadership. For example, if a state's department of education puts a certain school on its watch list because it is not making progress toward measures to fulfill the No Child Left Behind Act, some people might suggest that a work-centered leader is needed to take action and quickly move toward the designated goals. Others might suggest that a work-centered leader would do long-term damage to the morale of the faculty in such a situation, and a people-centered leader could be more successful. Because leadership studies have been done in so many different settings and with a variety of leaders, there is no conclusive evidence to suggest the superiority of one leadership style to another. Some teachers have experienced extreme leadership styles, while others have worked for administrators who have somehow combined both styles.

An understanding of leadership research allows teachers to develop a general sense of their administrators' management styles. This understanding can help teachers fulfill their responsibility for maintaining productive relationships with their administrators. In extreme situations, teachers may discover that building productive relationships with a particular administrator is very difficult, even close to impossible. In these cases, the teachers can in good conscience seek opportunities in other schools, fully aware of their ability to work with different leadership styles. The assessment shown in Table 6.1 will help you identify the characteristics of your administrator's leadership style.

The Leadership Assessment is meant to be a general indicator of your administrator's leadership style, based on your perceptions as a teacher. It is possible that your administrator can be described as equally work centered and people centered, according to the scores from the Leadership Assessment. Problems between you and your administrator are more likely to surface if you ranked your administrator higher for one style than the other. You can learn to improve communication with your school leader by learning about some common problems that arise when an administrator tends to display one style over the other.

Table 6.1   Leadership Assessment

Answer the questions based upon your first reaction after reading the question, using the following scale:

1 = *Strongly disagree*
2 = *Disagree*
3 = *Neutral*
4 = *Agree*
5 = *Strongly agree*

My Administrator...	1	2	3	4	5
1. Knows faculty and support staff on a personal basis					
2. Is very businesslike					
3. Is easily persuaded by vocal faculty members					
4. Is career driven and expects the same of the faculty					
5. Is well liked and very effective with people					
6. Is not afraid to make tough choices					
7. Tries to keep faculty informed of changes and decisions					
8. Moves the school toward achievement and is organized					

Instructions for scoring:
Add up scores for items 1, 3, 5, and 7.
Add up scores for items 2, 4, 6, and 8.

- If the score for items 1, 3, 5, and 7 fell between 10–20, your administrator exhibits characteristics consistent with a people-centered leadership style.
A higher score on these items indicates that your administrator has a stronger people-centered approach.

- If the score for items 2, 4, 6, and 8 fell between 10–20, your administrator exhibits characteristics consistent with a work-centered leadership style. A higher score on these items indicates that your administrator has a stronger work-centered approach.

The Work-Centered Administrator

There is no conclusive evidence that one leadership style is better than another or that leaders are predominately one personality type, but many leaders do share some common characteristics. Most administrators don't mind being in charge of the school—in fact, they like to be in charge and have sought leadership because they believe their ideas can make a difference. Anecdotally, these administrators would prefer to be in control rather than be controlled. In one assessment instrument developed by Rockhurst University (National Seminars Group, 2001), personality types are described along two dimensions: (1) the need to be around others, and (2) the need to be in control. Recapping from Chapter 2, the two personality types that most seek control are the Expressives and Drivers.

Work-centered administrators fit many of the descriptions of a Driver personality. They are serious, achievement oriented, and driven by accomplishment. They are focused on the task at hand and have high expectations of their faculty. Work-centered administrators are not afraid of a challenge, and they can help faculty and staff conquer a challenge as well. On the negative side, they may have little tolerance for mistakes and may lack the social finesse to solve interpersonal conflicts. These administrators invest a great amount of time at work, so it is difficult for them to take criticism or accept ideas that are different from their own.

There are some things that a teacher can do to build a productive work relationship with a work-centered administrator. First, it is important to remember that this leader is goal oriented and focused on specific objectives. As mentioned in Chapter 5, one criterion for a productive team is that all members must make an effort to understand the objective of the team and then decide whether they each agree with that objective. Teachers should look at the principal's objectives for the school and make sure they understand them. Then they can decide whether they agree with that direction.

The second action a teacher can take to build a productive work relationship with a work-centered administrator is to focus on the message and not the messenger. Relationships between administrators and teachers can easily be strained even if the teachers agree with the direction the administrator has outlined (the message). The problem lies in how the administrator communicates the message. A work-centered leader, focused on tasks and achievement, often neglects to address the thoughts, ideas, and feelings of those who are being asked to do the work or make the changes. Most everyone likes to be asked how they feel about a proposed objective and how they can contribute to its achievement. There is more likelihood that people will buy into an objective if they have been given the chance to talk about it—especially if their concerns are taken seriously. This is true even if the objectives have already been set. Discussion and feedback is especially important to those people who are attuned to relationships and feelings, which include the Expressive and Amiable personalities.

Administrators who are strongly work centered and have few people-centered attributes commonly announce changes and expect faculty and staff to start implementing them. Focus on the message and not the messenger if you agree with the administrator's objectives. Use your time and skills to contribute to the school, particularly on committees or in areas that you deem important. If you agree with the message but lack the resources, time, or training to contribute to the objectives, you must communicate with your administrator. There is a chance the administrator will think you are resisting the change, but there is also a chance that you have provided important feedback the administrator needs to hear. Or you can say nothing and do whatever is in your power to help the administrator reach the stated objectives for the school. This is not a bad strategy if you agree with the objectives and are willing to go above and beyond the call of duty. The risk of not saying anything is that you may perceive the demands of your job to be unreasonable and build resentment toward your administrator, the school, or the teaching profession. This risk is often present for those who feel unequipped to move toward the objectives or those who have not had the opportunity to provide feedback.

If you do not agree with the change, talk to other teachers to gauge their understanding of it and the reason for it. Try to talk to your administrator as well. If you still have a significant concern about it, you may need to find another school. If your concern is not significant enough to cause you to leave, realize that people hold different opinions in every work environment. A certain level of disagreement is going to happen from time to time, and some changes do involve personal discomfort.

The People-Centered Administrator

People-centered administrators possess strong human relation skills: Human relations skills enable a person to work with people, while technical skills enable a person to work with things (Katz, 1955). Strong people-centered administrators engender trust among their faculties because they take the time to talk to people and become attuned to the different needs of each teacher. The people-centered administrator first works to accommodate faculty and staff, while the work-centered administrator first focuses on the goals and objectives of the school.

People-centered administrators are not intimidated by new ideas or faculty input, and they tend to encourage participation, which can be viewed as a strength or a weakness. On the positive side, people like to provide feedback and have input into decisions. On the negative side, followers expect their leaders to be decisive and sure of themselves. A people-centered administrator who encourages participation and allows the group to make decisions and define objectives may be perceived as weak or overly susceptible to the influence of others. This may damage the administrator's credibility as a leader. People-centered leaders also have more difficulty establishing objectives than work-centered leaders. Building consensus takes time as the leader works to reconcile different opinions, but when the objectives are eventually established, there is widespread agreement.

Faculty should take advantage of the fact that relationships are important to people-centered administrators. Some faculty members may be as goal-oriented and job-focused as a work-centered administrator, but even these individuals should view casual conversations with the people-centered administrator as productive. It is through one-on-one conversation that the people-centered administrator learns of the needs, preferences, and concerns of individual faculty. This is an opportunity to build a productive work relationship and provide feedback as appropriate. People-centered administrators are amenable to gathering feedback.

A teacher can build a productive work relationship with a people-centered administrator by offering feedback but also by following through with suggestions that address a specific problem. Many people who work in a team do not mind contributing ideas, but they are hesitant to volunteer to do the work to make the idea happen. Faculty must be willing to help implement the ideas, whether the ideas come from the principal or a teacher. In one school, the principal, Mr. Raines, was an Amiable personality. Alice, a reading specialist in the school, had suggested that the faculty could use some training to learn how to work together as a team. Most teachers in the school were experienced faculty members. Mr. Raines felt that Alice's suggestion was important because the teachers were very independent and often had disagreements. Alice followed through with her suggestions and gave Mr. Raines the name of a local consultant, along with a description of the training modules he offered. Mr. Raines took the idea to the faculty, and there was overwhelming agreement that that training would be a valuable investment for the school.

Teachers are often in a position to help their administrators even if an initiative is already in progress. Dana is a high school teacher enrolled in a master's degree program at the local university. Dana solicited the help of one of her professors to help the school work out the details of its new organizational structure. The principal welcomed the help. The high school was transitioning to what is called a "dean's model," in which there are no assistant principals. There are several deans, and each dean is responsible for a group of students. The responsibilities include discipline and academic counseling, which is different from the previous model whereby one assistant was responsible for each of these areas for all students. The school felt that the dean's model was more personal for the students. In both the training and dean's model examples, teachers offered general suggestions but also helped move the idea to action. People-centered administrators usually welcome such help.

People-oriented administrators are sometimes willing to try new programs or ideas which may not have been thoroughly investigated. Teachers in this environment may feel like change is happening just for the sake of change. In these situations, it is important for teachers to ask questions or raise issues to determine whether the change is practical and beneficial to the school. For example, if one junior high has decided to shorten classes so that students attend seven classes in a day instead of six, does it make sense for another school to do the same thing? Your administrator may have heard about this change from his colleague and thought it might be worth trying in your school. Teachers can help determine whether this is an appropriate change for their school by raising questions that address the purpose of the change and the ability of the faculty to make the change. A teacher might even go the extra mile and find out whether the change has been successful in the other school or what problems surfaced from the change. In one school, faculty and staff agreed to go from six periods to seven, but unforeseen problems began to surface. The students did not have time to go to their lockers between classes anymore and had to carry all of their books around throughout the day. Teachers and administrators started getting complaints about heavy backpacks and aching muscles from parents. Though faculty had agreed to the change, an unexpected glitch surfaced during its implementation.

CONCLUSION

Leadership is an integral component of organizations. School-level administrators wear many hats as they interface with central administrators, board members, parents, faculty, and students. A principal has a responsibility to build a collegial environment and provide teachers with the climate and motivation they need to succeed. Teachers also share in the responsibility of building productive relationships within the school. Teachers who understand leadership styles can appreciate the strengths of their administrators and just as important, the weaknesses. This knowledge can help teachers work more effectively with their administrators, and it may also help them contribute to their schools in areas where their administrators are not strong.

CHAPTER SEVEN

Assessing Your Performance as a Teaching Professional

John always considered himself a very good teacher, but two years ago, his administrator evaluated him as needing improvement in several areas. At the time, John was not happy with the evaluation. He did not really believe his performance needed improvement. His emotional disbelief of the poor rating prevented him from looking at his contribution from the administrator's perspective.

Reflecting on his philosophy of what type of students he really wanted to help, however, John was able to assess more objectively that he was not fully committed to his job—half-hearted, on automatic, not fully engaged. He was able to see that a different school would be a better match for what he hoped to accomplish in teaching. John eventually asked his principal for a transfer to a school within the district that served more low-income students—a population that matters greatly to him.

Today, John is passionate about teaching high school math, and he feels comfortable with his colleagues and administrators. His evaluations have risen steadily, and he is eager to work with others when teachers are asked to assess new school initiatives or when the school faces unforeseen problems. Now, John is not only a good teacher, but his principal considers him a strong colleague. By his own admission, he is a better teacher today and readily contributes to the needs of the entire school. He enjoys working with his administration, other teachers, students, and the custodial and cafeteria staff.

Fortunately, it did not take John too long to consider his principal's feedback and honestly assess his own performance. As a teacher, you, too, should periodically conduct a self-assessment of your performance because it provides three important points of feedback: (1) an evaluation of your classroom performance, (2) an evaluation of your contribution and fit with your existing school, and (3) a view of how others perceive you, as a teacher and a colleague. Three general questions will help you assess your performance:

- How do I perceive my performance and contribution to the school?
- What is my potential for success teaching at this school?
- How do others perceive my performance and contribution to the school?

The next section provides some tools that will help you answer these questions in more detail.

TEACHER SELF-TEST AND ASSESSMENT PROFILE

Most of the literature that encourages professional self-improvement is strictly focused on administrators and managers. There are elements of some leadership models that are useful to employees not in administrative positions. Blanchard, Zigarmi, and Zigarmi (1985) developed a model that incorporates the development level of the employee. The model can be useful if employees understand their stages of development and the type of leadership they need as a result, but it was primarily intended to help leaders understand how to manage employees. Smith (1996) developed a concept somewhat similar to the Blanchard et al. (1985) model. Smith's framework of Will/Skill is geared toward helping people understand their ability to change based on their level of skill (ability) and will (motivation).

Together, Table 7.1 and Figure 7.1 make up a tool that I developed to help educators assess their own performance relative to their potential. It integrates several concepts from leadership and psychology (Bandura, 1997; Blanchard et al., 1985; Smith, 1996) but adapts them to education. The self-test in Table 7.1 helps you

Table 7.1   Self-Test for the Teacher Profile

Answer the following questions based upon your first reaction to them, using the following scale:

1 = *Strongly disagree*
2 = *Disagree*
3 = *Neutral*
4 = *Agree*
5 = *Strongly agree*

	1	2	3	4	5
1. Overall, I am successful and happy in my job.					
2. Others view me as competent.					
3. I have a high level of knowledge with regards to my job.					
4. My job evaluations from my administrator are strong.					
5. My abilities fit well with my job responsibilities.					
6. My administrator is effective.					
7. I get along well with fellow faculty.					
8. Outside issues unrelated to my job have not affected my performance in a significant way over the past six months.					

Instructions for scoring:

- Add up your total score for the assessment by adding all individual item scores.
- Your score should be between 8 and 40.
- If your score is between 32 to 40, your classification would be "Star Teacher."
- If your score is between 24 to 31, your classification would be "Work Bee Teacher."
- If your score is between 16 to 23, your classification would be "Problem Teacher."
- If your score is 15 or lower, your classification would be "Misplaced Professional."

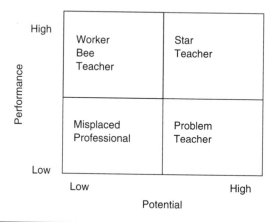

Figure 7.1   Teacher Assessment Profile

understand your performance and potential relative to your job as a teacher. As you take it, answer each question honestly, based on your first reaction. The test is compromised if you try to maximize the total score. The self-test is to be used with Figure 7.1, the Teacher Assessment Profile, which visually maps your potential versus performance. Your score on the self-test determines your placement on the Teacher Assessment Profile. Teachers can fall into one of four categories: Star Teacher, Worker Bee Teacher, Problem Teacher, or Misplaced Professional. The self-test is a guide to establish a benchmark for teacher performance and potential. There are many reasons a teacher may fall into a given profile, and there are many ways to move from one profile to another.

Star: Star Teachers are top performers. They have valuable knowledge, skills, abilities, and commitment to the school and are respected by peers and administrators. They display competence in the classroom and collegiality outside of it. Their mastery in the classroom is matched by their ability to work with others for the good of the entire school. Star Teachers usually have some degree of experience in education and can be strong mentors for new teachers.

A Star Teacher can continue to be one by looking for new challenges and learning opportunities. Without new challenges, the Star can become stagnant or bored, eventually becoming disinterested in teaching. Star Teachers who broaden their expertise and influence also maintain an interest in teaching and feel an ongoing responsibility for school success. This is accomplished by working with others to identify best practices, leading committee assignments, and helping to improve communication between administration and faculty. Star Teachers are excellent teachers, but they are also the people who make others feel like the school is a good place to work. These gems build collegiality within the school.

Worker Bee: Worker Bee Teachers have as their primary asset optimism and motivation. Much like the students who must work a bit harder to accomplish their goals, the Worker Bee Teacher must put in a little extra time to succeed. Worker Bees are usually open to feedback and direction. The extra effort the Worker Bee puts forth pays dividends because performance is still high.

Teachers who fit the Worker Bee profile are often new to the profession and need time to acculturate. They need training in the specifics of how their job is to be done, even though they may come with the general knowledge that was a desirable factor in their hiring. For example, learning about handling discipline is not quite the same as having to implement it in one's own classroom. It is also easy to get overwhelmed during the first few years, balancing course preparations and grading time with faculty meetings and special assignments. Perfecting this balancing act is a product of time, experience, and skill. In the end, the attributes of resolve and motivation are the Worker Bee's greatest strengths.

Worker Bees may also be those teachers who have not yet mastered their subject areas but are working hard to improve and showing positive results. Many teachers fall into this category. A 2002 study by The Education Trust, a Washington-based organization, found that in 1999–2000, about one in four secondary classes in core academic subjects were taught by teachers lacking at least a minor in the subject (Associated Press, 2002a). Although this issue raises substantial debate, the fact remains that many such teachers are in schools throughout the nation. If the assumption is that these teachers are working hard to make contributions, they may be Worker Bees. These teachers, like new teachers, need time and experience to absorb, master, and effectively relay the subject matter to students.

An important benefit of strong collegiality in a school is that new teachers—or teachers new to a subject—can find colleagues who are willing to lend a helping hand. Alice is a retired teacher who taught business-related classes during her tenure at a local Seattle high school. After fifteen years of teaching business classes, Alice was asked to teach an algebra course because of a pressing need in that area. Alice had a K–12 certificate that said she could teach any subject, but she did not feel confident teaching in this area. Alice did have positive working relationships with other teachers, and this earned her the support of several math teachers.

A person who may have formerly been a Star may become a Worker Bee if there has been a major change in the school. New instructional strategies, new course preparations, or even simple changes in scheduling require adjustment. The bigger the change, the more likely a Star will become a Worker Bee. This status is only temporary if the former Star is willing to learn and adapt. Training, mentoring, and constructive advice can help any Worker Bee become a Star. School collegiality is a prerequisite for these things. Without collegiality, it is very hard to provide the environment that Worker Bees need to become Star Teachers. If all teachers believed that they only needed to excel inside their individual classrooms for the school to succeed, the Worker Bees would never have the necessary support to reach their full potential.

Problem Teacher: Liz was a new teacher at Riverside Elementary school. She immediately became friends with a fourth grade teacher, Ellie, who introduced her to the school culture the first few days of orientation. During one informal tour, Ellie showed Liz the teacher's lounge. Ellie warned Liz to be careful about spending time there if Brett or Lisa were present. When Liz asked why, Ellie responded that the teacher's lounge was where Brett and Lisa liked to air complaints, talk about other teachers, and criticize administration. Brett and Lisa often stalled committee work or caused problems in faculty meetings. In many respects, they were Problem Teachers.

Problem Teachers are individuals who are not performing to their potential. The cause of Problem Teachers' difficulties is usually a certain level of discontent with other people or with themselves. It is possible that a Problem Teacher is just a chronic complainer who never sees the positive side of work or finds positive attributes in colleagues. In this case, the discontent is most attributed to the teacher's negative attitude, even if the capability is there to be a Star

Teacher. The behavior of a Problem Teacher erodes collegiality and has a negative effect on other teachers.

Negative feelings and attitudes are sometimes the result of how people interact with other colleagues or their administrators. There may be problems between teachers or between teachers and administrators. A group of women working in a preschool environment in Northern Arizona were very unhappy with their administrator. The administrator was very autocratic and would begin staff development sessions by circulating a sign-up sheet and explaining the sanctions for missing part of the training or taking too long for lunch. The administrator's management style was affecting faculty morale and motivation. The large number of Problem Teachers in this school was largely caused by negative administrative behavior.

Change can also be the source of discontent. Large changes may make Stars or Worker Bees feel like they are starting out all over again. They may become Problem Teachers when big changes are made and they have philosophical differences with the change, do not feel they have a stake in the new direction, or perceive that the change of course was imposed without appropriate notice.

Yet another reason capable teachers may not perform to their potential may simply be boredom or fatigue. These are the teachers who are in a rut. Problem Teachers who fit this mold often have several years of successful experience but reach a point of burnout. Teachers who do not seek new learning opportunities, either within the school or a professional association, could quickly become Problem Teachers. Professional activity provides new opportunities for continuing development of skills as well as contribution to the classroom, the department, and the school. A teacher who contributes to school collegiality is likely involved in schoolwide initiatives and professional growth. This combination is a sure antidote to boredom or burnout.

Last, Problem Teachers may be experiencing personal problems that are affecting the work environment. Alnutt (1982) has said that human beings are twenty-four-hour-a-day people, possessing only one brain with which to control all their activities, and this brain has to cover both work and play. Events in one part of life may influence events in another, meaning that challenges or problems at home often affect work. Teachers experience problems just like everybody else: child issues, divorce, a death in the family, or personal money problems. Such crises can cause short-term performance problems.

If the lowered performance persists, then a counseling or professional intervention may be necessary.

Problem Teachers need support. The potential for performance exists, but it needs some external attention to be realized. An encouraging colleague may help turn the Problem Employee into a Worker Bee or a Star. If Problem Teachers work in an environment where teacher collegiality is high, it is likely that they will find the support they need.

Misplaced Professional: Most administrators and veteran teachers have lived through the experience of inheriting a well-traveled transfer teacher. In some situations, a transfer teacher may not have been a proper match with a previous school. John, the teacher in the beginning of this chapter, got along with his colleagues and administrator, but his desire was to work in a place where he felt he could impact minority children. John could have easily and mistakenly been characterized as a Misplaced Professional. The good news is that a transfer was the answer to John's problems. Once in a new school environment, he thrived, and he is now a Star Teacher.

There are those teachers who have transferred multiple times and still have problems. In other cases, the teacher has worked in the profession for a few years but has simply not been successful. These people may be Misplaced Professionals, not meant to be teachers. This may be a factor in today's climate when nearly half of new teachers quit after just five years and a third quit after three years (Thomas, 2002). Not all of them are Misplaced Professionals, but it is likely that some percentage of them would be happier in another profession. Keeping Misplaced Professionals in the classroom and in the school because there is a shortage probably does more harm than good. Retaining a Misplaced Professional could mean ongoing problems for the person, other teachers, administrators, and, most important, the students.

A teacher may temporarily be a Misplaced Professional for several valid reasons. Many of these reasons are similar to those that make a teacher a Problem Teacher: personal problems, change in job assignments, or miscommunication with management. Misplaced Professionals who are experiencing temporary problems often need support, just as does the Problem Teacher. An encouraging colleague or administrator may help the Misplaced Professional become a Worker Bee and perhaps even a Star.

If Misplaced Professionals work in environments where collegiality is high, the chances of transforming into a Worker Bee are high. If they are given support and have a collegial environment but are still unable to contribute, it is likely that they are not a match for the teaching profession. If they work in an environment where collegiality is low, they are likely to remain misplaced and unhappy, causing problems in the classroom and in the school.

USING THE TEACHER ASSESSMENT PROFILE AS A TOOL FOR IMPROVEMENT

The Teacher Assessment Profile is an indicator of current performance relative to potential. If you are currently a Worker Bee and hope to become a Star, then you must identify some goals. Bandura's (1997) seminal work on self-efficacy provides compelling evidence that our thoughts and expectations influence the outcomes we produce—our goal achievement. The Teacher Assessment Profile is an opportunity to chart the outcomes you are producing against the outcomes you hope to achieve. Even if you are a Star, there is still room for growth.

Identifying an improvement goal is an important step to growth since you build skills as you achieve your goals. Consider a skill that most teachers need to some degree: effective speaking. Some people seem to have the confidence and ability to hold an audience captive; others need improvement in this area. Jennifer liked teaching but didn't really think she had the presentation skills to be a top teacher. She was a very reserved person and considered herself a Worker Bee. She wanted to improve her speaking skills and took steps to accomplish that goal:

She enrolled in a seminar for improving presentation skills.

She took graduate courses where presentations were required.

She has learned how her already excellent listening skills could actually help her respond (speak) to people more effectively since she clearly understands what they are saying.

By assessing her own performance and working to get better, Jennifer has grown as a teacher. She set some goals and took steps to achieve them, and today she feels more confident teaching her middle school students and offering input at staff meetings. Jennifer improved her speaking skills, and it has made a difference in how she feels about her job.

CONCLUSION

Teachers are capable of moving from one profile to another. The value of the Teacher Assessment Profile is that it tells you about your performance today and raises some questions about your potential for the future. Along with the self-test and the Teacher Assessment Profile in this chapter, there are four questions that, if honestly and periodically addressed, will help you maintain an accurate evaluation of your performance:

> How at this time do I classify myself, according to the Teacher Assessment Profile?

> How would my administrator classify me, according to the Teacher Assessment Profile?

> How would my colleagues classify me, according to the Teacher Assessment Profile?

> Is there a difference between how I classify myself and how others would classify me?

CHAPTER EIGHT

Working Together

Rose is a second grade teacher and previously worked in an elementary school in a large urban area. The school prided itself on teacher collegiality because of the strong relationships among the teachers and the level of trust the principal had built with the faculty. The school culture was predicated on teachers sharing best practices and working together. The school's improving accountability measures coincided with the faculty's growing focus on teacher collegiality. Just as the school seemed to be functioning smoothly, the principal was rotated to another school within the district. Rose followed her principal to the new school, with both expecting to pick up where they had left off in their old school.

Rose and her principal soon found that teachers in the new school did not talk to each other very often. These teachers were more likely to interpret input, suggestions, and best practice discussions as criticism against their personal teaching methods. They had never worked in an environment where they had to communicate or even get along. Sadly, Rose and her principal found that existing cultures and attitudes are hard to change. In fairness to the teachers, Rose's principal was asking them to do something they did not know how to do, so they naturally resisted. They had no idea what collegiality meant and how it could help improve the school. The teachers had never engaged in a discussion about the value of the dialogue that Rose and her principal were used to, nor had the teachers received any sort of training to help them learn to work in teams or settle conflicts and disagreements.

As Rose found out, the strength of collegiality in schools depends on how well teachers work together and with their administrators.

A school principal cannot build or maintain a collegial school environment alone; it requires the efforts and contributions of individual teachers. Positive relationships do not happen automatically—they require sustained effort.

As you have progressed through this book, you have gathered some powerful tools with which you can build a healthy and nurturing environment in your school—or keep a good one that way. Let's briefly review the underlying themes of each chapter so that you can see how the various tools help to create successful schools and successful teachers.

KNOWING YOURSELF

People who have positive working relationships know their own strengths and weaknesses. Since school collegiality is about effective relationships with others, the first step to improve working relationships requires that you examine your own qualities: those that positively and negatively influence others. This self-examination is critical because it provides a foundation for how you view yourself, which influences how you interact with others. In Chapter 2, you found tools that helped you define your personal leadership qualities and how they influence school collegiality.

IMPROVING COLLEGIALITY

It is important for teachers to assess themselves, but it is equally important to be familiar with some effective tools to build positive working relationships with others. Chapters 3 through 6 are application oriented and introduced some of these tools to help you improve school collegiality. The thread that runs through these chapters is communication. The goal of all teachings on personality and conflict types is to enhance communication between individuals, which also improves team effectiveness. The probability that you can settle conflicts without administrative involvement is greatly enhanced now that you understand the sources of conflict and various strategies that help resolve it. Your ability to work on a team and make a productive contribution has also been strengthened by learning about team dynamics and the value that different individuals bring to the problem-solving process.

UNDERSTANDING LEADERSHIP STYLES

Knowing about different administrative leadership styles will specifically improve your working relationships with your administrators. And that leads to viewing your workplace in a positive light. You share the responsibility for the quality of the relationship with your administrator, and you will improve communication if you understand different administrative leadership styles. Administrators, like teachers, have different personalities and different ways of resolving conflict. Using the assessment in Chapter 6, you can now understand how your administrators lead. Combining this knowledge with insight into your own personality type gives you another tool to help you effectively communicate with the leaders in your school.

As you have learned about your personality, your way of approaching and resolving conflict, and your role in working with a team, it is also important to assess these personal attributes against your job performance. All of these things contribute to your performance, for better or worse. The self-assessment in Chapter 7 gave you an opportunity to look at your performance from your perspective and the perspective of others. By doing this, you can reflect on every element of your performance, which includes your work inside and outside the classroom. And it allows you to more clearly align yourself with what matters most to you and to determine whether that is available in your present situation.

CONCLUSION

In the end, the measure of individual success you experience as a teacher is dependent on the quality of your teaching and the quality of your working relationships. These two areas affect one another and the success of your school. I sincerely hope that *Teachers Working Together for School Success* has helped and will continue to help you improve how you work with other teachers and administrators and amplify the satisfaction you get from this honorable and vital profession.

References

Alnutt, M. (1982). Human factors: Basic principles. In R. Hurst, & L. R. Hurst (Eds.), *Pilot error* (2nd ed., pp. 1-22). Northvale, NJ: Jason Aronson.

Aronson, E. (1992). *The social animal* (6th ed.). New York: Freeman.

Associated Press. (2002a, August 25). Many teach outside subject. *Las Cruces Sun News,* p. A4.

Associated Press. (2002b). *U.S. teachers log most hours.* Retrieved February 3, 2004, from www.cnn.com/2002/EDUCATION/10/30/us. education.comparison.ap/index.html

Associated Press. (January 13, 2003). *White teachers fleeing black schools.* Retrieved February 3, 2004, from www.cnn.com/2003/EDUCATION/01/13/resegregation.teachers.ap/index.html

Bandura, A. (1997). *Self-efficacy: The exercise of control.* New York: Freeman.

Basadur, M. (1995). *The power of innovation.* London, UK: Pittman.

Blake, R. R., & Mouton, J. S. (1964). *The managerial grid.* Houston, TX: Gulf.

Blanchard, K. H. (1985). *SLII: A situational approach to managing people.* Escondido, CA: Blanchard Training and Development.

Blanchard, K., Zigarmi, P., & Zigarmi, D. (1985). Leadership and the one minute manager: Increasing effectiveness through situational leadership. New York: William Morrow.

Buckingham, M., & Coffman, C. (1999). *First break all the rules.* New York: Simon & Schuster.

Carlyle, T. (1994). On heroes, hero worship, and heroic in history. In R. Heifetz, *Leadership without easy answers,* p. 16. Cambridge, MA: Harvard Business Press. (Original document published in 1841)

Cox, T. (2003). Cultural diversity in organizations: Intergroup conflict. In J. S. Ott, S. J. Parkes, & R. B. Simpson (Eds.), *Classic readings in organizational behavior* (3rd ed., p. 263). Belmont, CA: Wadsworth. (Original work published 1993)

Evans, R. (1996). *The human side of school change.* San Francisco: Jossey-Bass.

Fiedler, F. E., & Chemers, M. M. (1974). *Improving leadership effectiveness: The leader match concept* (2nd ed.). New York: John Wiley.

Fisher, R., & Ury, W. (1981). *Getting to yes: Negotiating agreement without giving in.* New York: Penguin.

Fullan, M. (2001). *Leading in a culture of change.* San Francisco: Jossey-Bass.

Goodstein, L. D., & Burke, W. W. (1995). Creating successful organizational change. In W. W. Burke (Ed.), *Managing organizational change.* New York: American Management Association.

Hackman, R. J., & Oldman, G. R. (2000). The design of work groups and groups for work. In S. J. Ott (Ed.), *Classic readings in organizational behavior* (2nd ed., p. 256). Belmont, CA: Wadsworth. (Original work published 1980)

Handy, C. (1994). *Age of paradox.* Cambridge, MA: Harvard Business Press.

Heifetz, R. (1994). *Leadership without easy answers.* Cambridge, MA: Harvard Business Press.

Hendricks, W. (1991). *How to manage conflict.* Overland Park, KS: National Press Publications.

Hunt, M. (1993). *The story of psychology.* New York: Doubleday.

Katz, R. L. (1955, January-February). *Skills of an effective administrator.* Cambridge, MA: Harvard Business Review.

LaHaye, T. (1984). *Why you act the way you do.* Wheaton, IL: Living Books, Tyndale House.

Maslow, A. (2000). A theory of motivation. In S. J. Ott (Ed.), *Classic readings in organizational behavior* (2nd ed., p. 45). Belmont, CA: Wadsworth. (Original work published in 1943)

Maxwell, J. (1998). *Developing the leader within you.* Nashville, TN: Thomas Nelson.

McGregor, D. M. (1957). The human side of enterprise. *Management Review.* New York: American Management Association.

McLaughlin, M., & Talbert, J. (2001). Professional communities and the work of high-school teaching. In M. Fullan, *Leading in a culture of change,* pp. 64-67. San Francisco: Jossey-Bass.

National Seminars Group. (2001). *Management and leadership skills for first time managers and supervisor* [Training booklet]. Shawnee Mission, KS: Rockhurst University, Author.

Olson, M. (1965). *The logic of collective action: Public goods and the theory of groups.* Cambridge, MA: Harvard University Press.

Roethlisberger, F. J. (2003). Management and morale. In J. S. Ott, S. J. Parkes, & R. B. Simpson (Eds.), *Classic readings in organizational behavior* (3rd ed., p.142). Belmont, CA: Wadsworth. (Original work published 1969)